Boost Your Spelling Power

Published by :
Lotus Press Publishers & Distributors

Boost Your Spelling Power

M. Thomas

Lotus
PRESS

4735/22, Prakash Deep Building
Ansari Road, Darya Ganj,
New Delhi - 110002

Lotus Press : Publishers & Distributors
Unit No. 220, 2nd Floor, 4735/22, Prakash Deep Building,
Ansari Road, Darya Ganj, New Delhi- 110002
Ph.: 23280047, 98118-38000
• E-mail : lotuspress1984@gmail.com
www.lotuspress.co.in

Boost Your Spelling Power

ISBN: 81-8382-128-6

Printed & Published by : **Lotus Press Publisher & Distributors,** New Delhi-02

PREFACE

The most important language of all that holds international significance, English has a richness of words that increase in number almost every year. The more the number of words in it, the more difficult it is to get comfortable with their spellings. However, spellings are important, as they are needed to be correct not just for getting good grades, but they also to avoid any undesirable impression on the reader.

The difficulty most people face while remembering spellings is that there are at least 1,100 different ways to spell. In addition to this, English language has 44 different sounds. A key to remembering spellings of words is to break them up according to sound and then spell them.

Apart from that, there are certain words that are spelled differently in different countries. The present book is a guide for improving spellings in the easiest possible manner. The rules and tips suggested herein are directed towards making the task of learning spelling easy and logical.

Apart from becoming familiar with the basic fundamentals of English spellings, the book also gives the readers a chance to know more about the intricate details of rules of spellings and the exceptions that follow. Examples accompany each and every concept explained that aid in the understanding of the reader.

Hope the readers find the book of use and are able to derive bits of knowledge from it.

Author

CONTENTS

CHAPTER 1

Introduction to Spellings

Writing is a representation of the spoken word. It is here that spellings start to matter. The accents and pronunciation can change easily and quickly. However, what is written in books and dictionaries remains static for years. English language has a myriad of words. Learning spellings of each one of them is indeed a tough task. We remember spellings of only those words that we happen to use regularly. However, it is extremely important to learn to spell correctly, because:

- Poor spelling is the first thing a reader notices.
- Poor spelling creates a bad impression.
- Examiners, teachers, prospective employers, etc. often place undue weight on spellings.
- Anxiety about spelling may inhibit your writing, especially your choice of words.

To improve and develop spelling power, you need to:

- Develop an interest in words.
- Feel comfortable while using new words.
- Learn about the way words are built up using syllables.

The Importance of Syllables in Spellings

Good spellers start with breaking words up into syllables. Syllables are the individual sounds that make up a word.

For example, consider the words Careful, Natural and

University. They can be broken into syllables as follows:

- care - ful
- nat - u - ral
- u - ni - vers - i- ty

Breaking a word into syllables makes it easier to deal with one small bit at a time.

Now, read aloud each of the following words and then read them broken into syllables. You will find it easy to memorise the spellings of these words once you are comfortable with breaking words into syllables and pronouncing them thus.

Word	**Syllables**
Probably	prob•a•bly
Gentleman	gen•tle•man
Sideways	side•ways
Impossible	im•pos•si•ble
Themselves	them•selves
Ordinary	or•di•nar•y
Scramble	scram•ble
Wondering	won•der•ing
Neither	nei•ther
Problem	prob•lem
Shampoo	sham•poo
Nowadays	now • a • days
Autobiography	au•to•bi•og•ra•phy
Spoonful	spoon•ful
Intercontinental	in•ter•con•ti•nen•tal
Conniving	con•_niv•ing

Encourage	en•cour•age
Comporting	com•port•ing
Jurisdiction	ju•ris•dic•tion
Cerebral	ce•re•bral

Improving Spellings with Consonant Blends

Sometimes you're not sure how to spell a word and you need to look it up in a dictionary to find how to spell it right. If you can work out the first syllable, you stand a good chance of finding the word. Some words start with a consonant blend. This is where two or more consonants run into one another or **blend** together. Have a look at some examples.

Read aloud these words:

blanket **pl**astic **tr**eat **str**ipe **gr**and

Consonant blends are often difficult to hear so you need to say the words very clearly.

If you make lists of words starting with these blends, you will get used to hearing them and will be able to recognise the patterns.

Have a look at some more consonant blends:

- blunder
- broken
- climate
- cracker
- dreadful
- flood
- fridge
- globe
- group
- platform
- protect
- scorch
- scratch
- shred
- shriek
- sketch
- slippery
- smoke
- snooze
- special

- splendid
- sprinkle
- squeeze
- statue
- struggle

Working with Vowels

English language has a, e, i, o, u as vowels. Vowels are speech sounds produced without occluding, diverting, or obstructing the flow of air from the lungs.

The vowel 'e' is the magic alphabet. Read out the following words aloud. Notice how the 'e' affects the way the previous vowel is said.

• cap • cape • slop • slope

The way we say the -a- in cape is different to the way that we say it in cap. This is because of the vowel e.

Long vowel sound: -a-

The long -a- is most often written a-e, for example st<u>ate</u>. Usually there is only one letter between the a and the e as in pl<u>ate</u>. However, often there is more than one, as in t<u>able</u>. It's the magic e which makes the -a- have a long sound.

Carefully observe the a-e combination in each of the following words:

- bracelet
- cradle
- dazed
- disgraceful
- displacement
- grade
- hate
- ladle
- mate
- obstacle
- parade
- rotate
- skate
- speculate
- statement
- trace

At the same time, **-ai-** and **-ay** also make the long 'a' sound. You'll notice that **-ai-** usually comes in the **middle** of a word and the long 'a' right at the **end** of a word is always **-ay**. Observe the **-ai-** and **-ay** in the following words:

- available
- decay
- exclaim
- railway
- sway
- yesterday
- clay
- drain
- maintain
- swain
- trailer

Long vowel sound: -e-

When you hear a long -e- , particularly in the middle of a word, it's often spelled -ea- or -ee-. Have a look at some of the examples:

- between
- freezing
- keep
- loudspeaker
- proceed
- revealed
- sweetness
- cheap
- green
- leaf
- meal
- reason
- steal
- wheel

Long vowel sound: -i-

As is usual with long vowel sounds, most long -i- sounds are written using the vowel e. For example:

- bridle
- decided
- entitled
- fine
- deadline
- dynamite
- fertile
- lively

- mice
- miserly
- quite
- silent
- stalactite
- title
- trifle
- untimely
- write

However, **-igh-** and **-y** also make the long 'i' sound. **-igh** is usually found in the **middle** of a word and the long 'i' right at the **end** of a word is nearly always **-y**.

Carefully observe the **-igh-** and --**y** in the following words:

- apply
- bright
- delight
- midnight
- moonlight
- nightfall
- reply
- supply
- terrify
- tight

Long vowel sound: -o-

As is usual with other long vowel sounds, most long -o- sounds are written using the magic e.

Have a look at the o-e pattern in the following words:

- coke
- dozed
- homework
- lonely
- poker
- rodent
- slope
- stolen
- stonemason
- stove
- telephone

However, **-oa-** and **-ow-** also make the long 'o' sound. **-oa-** is usually found in the **middle** of a word and the long 'o' right at the **end** of a word is nearly always **-ow**. Read out aloud the following words:

- borrow
- elbow
- foaming
- goal
- narrow
- coastguard
- float
- follow
- know
- roadwork

Using the Apostrophe Mark

The apostrophe is used above a word for two reasons:–

- To depict ownership, as in:–
  - **Ratan's ball** – here the ball belongs to Ratan so the apostrophe goes after Ratan.
  - The **men's parlour** – here the parlour belongs to all the men, so the apostrophe goes after men.
- To depict that one or more letters are missing, as in:–
  - **We've** brought a new cycle for the little boy – here the apostrophe shows that **ha** is missing from **We have.**
  - **She'll go** to school next month- here the apostrophe shows that **wi** is missing from **She will.**

Have a look at the following words with the apostrophe mark:

- could have could've
- do not don't
- does not doesn't
- he will he'll
- it is it's
- let us let's
- should not shouldn't
- we have we've

- will not — won't
- would not — wouldn't

Strategies for Memorising Spellings

Whenever you come across a new word always use the **LOOK - THINK - COVER - WRITE - CHECK** method to memorise its spelling.

- **LOOK** carefully at the new word. See how you can break it into smaller bits. Do any of the smaller bits remind you of the patterns of letters from other words?
- **THINK** about the parts of the words which might cause problems – double letters for instance, or a vowel that isn't pronounced as you would expect.
- **COVER** the word and close your eyes. Try to see it in your mind's eye.
- **WRITE** the word down without looking back.
- **CHECK** to see if you're right. If not, look carefully at where you went wrong and try again.

CHAPTER 2

Rules to Remember

At times English spellings often appear to be totally illogical. Have a look at some important rules that would help you to decode the mysteries of English spelling. However, always remember, even the best rules have their exceptions:

Using -er/est

The comparative or superlative forms of short adjective words are made by adding -er or -est.

The Rule Says

Add **-er** or **-est** at the end of the adjective, as in:

- great > greater > greatest
- kind > kinder > kindest
- near > nearer > nearest
- quick > quicker > quickest

Exceptions

If the adjective ends in:	What to do:	Add:	Example:
Consonant & -y	Change the -y to -i	-er or est	happy > happier > happiest
Consonant & -e	Remove the -e	-er or est	late > later > latest

Consonant + vowel+ consonant	Double the last letter	-er or est	hot > hotter > hottest

Note: Adjectives ending in -l are regular, except in:

cruel > crueller > cruelest

Using -ing/-ed

We often add -ing or -ed to a verb to make other forms of the verb. For example:

The girl was *walking* when it *started raining*.

The Rule Says

Add -ing or -ed at the end of the base verb:

- open > opening > opened
- play > playing > played
- work > working > worked

Exceptions

If the base verb ends in:	What to do:	Add:	Example:
Consonant + vowel + consonant and a stressed syllable	Double the final consonant	-ing or -ed	flip > flipping > flipped map > mapping > mapped However, open > opening >opened (Since there is no stress on last syllable)
Consonant & -e	Remove the -e	-ing or -ed	dance > dancing > danced dye > dying > dyed make > making

			phone > phoning > phoned rake > raking > raked
-ie	Change the -ie to -y	-ing or -d	die > dying > died lie > lying > lied

Using –ly

Often, we make an adverb by adding -ly to an adjective. For example, neat > neatly.

The Rule Says

Add -ly at the end of the adjective. For example:

- bare > barely
- beautiful > beautifully
- coy > coyly
- intelligent > intelligently
- loud > loudly
- quick > quickly
- senseless > senselessly

Exceptions

If the adjective ends in:	What to do:	Add:	Example:
-ll	Nothing	-y	full > fully
Consonant & -le	Remove the final	-e-y	terrible > terribly
-y (except in one syllable adjectives)	remove the -y	-ily	happy > happily

Note: One syllable adjectives ending in -y are regular, except:

- day > daily
- gay > gaily

Spelling Final 'y' before a Suffix

If a word ends in 'y' preceded by a consonant, change the 'y' to 'i' before adding the suffix.

For example:

- curly > curlier, curliest
- party > parties
- thirty > thirties, thirtieth

However, if the suffix already begins with 'i', keep the 'y' (except before the suffix '-ise'):

For example:

- agony > agonise
- fry > frying
- memory > memorise
- party > partying

When the ending 'y' is preceded by a vowel ('a', 'e', 'i', 'o' or 'u'), 'y' does not change to 'i'.

For example:

- journey > journeying
- trolley > trolleys

Final Silent 'e'

If a word ends in a consonant followed by a silent 'e', drop the 'e' before the endings beginning with a vowel. However, keep the 'e' before endings beginning with a consonant.

For example:

- care > caring > careful
- engage > engaging > engagement
- fate > fatal > fateful
- scarce > scarcity > scarcely

Spelling Words with Double Consonants

Double the final consonant before a suffix beginning with a vowel if the following two conditions are true:

- The consonant ends a stressed syllable or a one-syllable word.
- The consonant is preceded by a single vowel.

For example:

- drag > dragged, dragged
- wet > wetter, wettest, wetting
- occur > occurred, occurring
- refer > referral, referring

Adding –s

'-s' is added to words in two conditions:

- To make plural nouns, for example, boy > boys.
- To form the 3rd person singular of the present simple tense, for example, I play > you play > she plays.

The Rule Says

Just add -s at the end of the word. For example:

- demand > demands
- fail > fails
- take > takes
- dog > dogs
- play > plays

Exceptions

If the word ends in:	What to do:	Add:	Example:
-x	Nothing	-es	box > boxes
-sh	Nothing	-es	brush > brushes
-z	Nothing	-es	chintz > chintzes
-ch	Nothing	-es	church > churches

-ss	Nothing	-es	fax > faxes mass > masses
-f or -fe	Remove the -f or -fe	-ves	wife > wives calf > calves Except in: belief > beliefs chief > chiefs dwarf > dwarfs gulf > gulfs proof > proofs roof > roofs
Consonant & -y	Remove the -y	-ies	baby > babies spy > spies

Note: Words that end in -o normally just add s, except in:

- buffalo > buffaloes
- cargo > cargoes
- domino > dominoes
- echo > echoes
- go > goes
- grotto > grottoes
- halo > haloes
- hero > heroes
- mango > mangoes
- mosquito > mosquitoes
- motto > mottoes (or mottos)
- potato > potatoes
- tomato > tomatoes
- tornado > tornadoes
- torpedo > torpedoes
- veto > vetoes
- volcano > volcanoes

Is it '-ible' or '-able'?

Many words end in -ible and -able. At times it becomes difficult to remember which spelling to use.

-ible Ending

The -ible ending is for words of Latin origin. There are about 180 words ending in -ible. Except these 180 words, new words are being created with -ible ending. Here are the most common examples:

Few words ending in –ible

accessible	admissible
audible	collapsible
combustible	compatible
comprehensible	contemptible
credible	defensible
destructible	digestible
divisible	edible
fallible	flexible
gullible	horrible
illegible	implausible
inaccessible	incontrovertible
incredible	indefensible
indelible	inedible
insensible	intelligible
invincible	invisible
irresistible	irreversible
ostensible	permissible
plausible	possible

responsible
reversible
sensible
susceptible
suggestible
tangible
terrible
visible

-able Ending

The '-able' ending is for non-Latin words. It is also used for forming new words.

Few Words ending in –able

abatable
abdicable
abolishable
abominable
absorbable
accruable
achievable
acquirable
actable
actionable
adaptable
addable
addressable
adjustable
admirable
adoptable
adorable
advisable
affable
affirmable
affordable
agreeable
allowable
alterable
amenable
amendable
amiable
amicable
anticipatable
applicable
arguable
ascendable
atonable
attachable
attainable
attemptable
attributable
auditable

available
avowable
awardable
bearable
beatable
believable
bendable
bitable
bleachable
bondable
bootable
breakable
breathable
bribable
cable calculable
callable
cancelable
capable
cartable
cashable
causable
censurable
certifiable
chargeable
charitable
checkable
chewable
classifiable
cleanable
clearable
closeable
clubbable
cognizable
coinable
collectable
commensurable
communicable
companionable
comparable
compassable
compensable
computable
conceivable
condonable
confirmable
conformable
conscionable
constable
consumable
contestable
contradictable
copyrightable
correctable
coverable
covetable

creditable	crunchable
crushable	culpable
damnable	danceable
datable	dateable
decasyllable	decidable
decipherable	declarable
defendable	deferrable
deflectable	deformable
defrayable	degradable
delegable	deliverable
demonstrable	demountable
deniable	dependable
deplorable	deportable
describable	desirable
despicable	detestable
developable	diminishable
dimmable	disable
discountable	discreditable
displaceable	displayable
disprovable	disputable
doable	doubtable
downloadable	drillable
drinkable	dubitable
eatable	editable
educable	effable
effaceable	embraceable
emendable	employable

endurable	enforceable
enjoyable	enlargeable
enumerable	enviable
equable	erasable
erectable	evitable
evocable	evolvable
exactable	examinable
exceptionable	exchangeable
excusable	extraditable
extricable	fable
faceable	factorable
falsifiable	farmable
fashionable	fathomable
fatigable	favourable
fellable	fermentable
fertilisable	fineable
fixable	flammable
flappable	flushable
flyable	foldable
fordable	formidable
friable	gable
generable	getable
governable	gradable
grantable	graspable
guessable	guidable
habitable	harvestable
healable	hearable

helpable
heritable
hirable
honourable
hospitable
huggable
identifiable
ignitable
ignorable
illaudable
illimitable
illuminable
imaginable
imitable
immeasurable
immedicable
immensurable
immitigable
immovable
immutable
impalpable
impassable
impeachable
impeccable
impenetrable
imperishable
impermeable
imperturbable
implacable
implantable
imponderable
importable
impracticable
impregnable
impressionable
improbable
improvable
imputable
inadvisable
inalienable
inalterable
inappeasable
inapplicable
inappreciable
inapproachable
inarguable
incalculable
incapable
inclinable
includable
incommensurable
incommunicable
incomparable
incomputable

inconceivable	inconsiderable
inconsolable	inconsumable
incontestable	incontrollable
incorporable	increasable
inculpable	incurable
indecipherable	indeclinable
indecomposable	indefatigable
indefinable	indemonstrable
indescribable	indeterminable
indictable	indiscoverable
indispensable	indisputable
indistinguishable	indomitable
indubitable	ineffable
ineffaceable	ineluctable
inenarrable	inequitable
ineradicable	inescapable
inestimable	inevitable
inexcusable	inexorable
inexpiable	inexplicable
inexpugnable	inextinguishable
inextricable	inferable
inflammable	inflatable
inhabitable	inheritable
inhospitable	inimitable
innumerable	inoperable
insatiable	inscrutable
inseparable	insolvable

instable	insufferable
insuperable	insupportable
insurable	insurmountable
interchangeable	interminable
interoperable	interpretable
intersubstitutable	intolerable
intractable	invaluable
invariable	inviolable
invulnerable	irreclaimable
irreconcilable	irrecoverable
irredeemable	irrefragable
irremovable	irreparable
irreplaceable	irreproachable
irresolvable	irretrievable
irrevocable	irritable
isolable	isolatable
joinable	justifiable
kickable	kissable
knowable	knowledgeable
lamentable	lapsable
laudable	laughable
learnable	liable
licensable	likable
likeable	limitable
listenable	litigable
livable	localisable
locatable	lockable

losable
lovable
loveable
maintainable
malleable
manageable
maneuverable
marketable
marriageable
measurable
memorable
mentionable
merchantable
microwavable
miserable
mistakable
mixable
modifiable
moldable
monosyllable
mountable
movable
moveable
multivariable
mutable
nameable
navigable
negotiable
nonexpendable
nonflammable
noninflammable
nonmalleable
nonnegotiable
nonperishable
nonrefundable
nonrenewable
nontaxable
nontransferable
nonviable
notable
noticeable
numerable
objectionable
observable
obtainable
operable
opposable
orderable
palatable
palpable
parable
pardonable
passable
patentable

payable
peaceable
penetrable
perceivable
perdurable
performable
perishable
permeable
permutable
personable
persuadable
photodegradable
pitiable
playable
pleasurable
pliable
polysyllable
portable
potable
predicable
predictable
preferable
pregnable
presentable
presumable
preventable
printable
probable
procurable
profitable
programmable
pronounceable
prosecutable
publishable
punishable
purchasable
quantifiable
quenchable
questionable
quotable
ratable
reachable
readable
realisable
reasonable
recallable
receivable
rechargeable
reclaimable
recognisable
recommendable
reconcilable
reconfigurable
recordable

recoupable recoverable
rectifiable recyclable
redeemable redoubtable
referable refillable
refundable refutable
regrettable reimbursable
relatable releasable
reliable relievable
remarkable remediable
remittable renegotiable
renewable rentable
repairable reparable
repayable repeatable
replaceable replicable
reportable reproachable
reprogrammable reputable
resalable researchable
resolvable respectable
restorable retable
retractable retrievable
returnable reusable
revisable revivable
revocable roundtable
sable sailable
saleable salvable
salvageable satiable
savable scalable

sealable
searchable
seasonable
seeable
selectable
sellable
separable
servable
serviceable
severable
shapeable
shareable
shrinkable
sinkable
sizeable
sliceable
sociable
solvable
specifiable
spoilable
squeezable
stable
stackable
stainable
stoppable
storable
stretchable
strippable
substitutable
subsumable
sufferable
suitable
supportable
supposable
surmountable
survivable
sustainable
swayable
syllable
table
tamable
taxable
teachable
tenantable
terminable
testable
thinkable
tillable
timetable
tolerable
touchable
traceable
tractable
tradable

trafficable	trainable
transferable	transformable
translatable	transmittable
transmutable	transplantable
transportable	transposable
traversable	treasonable
treatable	trustable
tunable	turntable
unable	unacceptable
unaccountable	unaffordable
unalienable	unalterable
unanswerable	unappeasable
unapproachable	unarguable
unassailable	unattainable
unavailable	unavoidable
unbearable	unbeatable
unbelievable	unbendable
unbreakable	unbridgeable
unburnable	unchallengeable
unchangeable	uncharitable
unclassifiable	uncomfortable
unconceivable	unconformable
unconquerable	unconscionable
uncontainable	uncontrollable
uncorrectable	uncountable
uncultivable	undecipherable
undeliverable	undeniable

undependable	understandable
undesirable	undetectable
undeterminable	undiscoverable
undisputable	undoable
undrinkable	uneatable
uneducable	unelectable
unemployable	unendurable
unenforceable	unenviable
unexceptionable	unexcitable
unexplainable	unfashionable
unfathomable	unfavourable
unflappable	unforeseeable
unforgettable	unforgivable
ungovernable	ungraspable
unidentifiable	unimpeachable
uninhabitable	uninsurable
unjustifiable	unknowable
unknowledgeable	unlikable
unlivable	unlovable
unmanageable	unmarketable
unmatchable	unmemorable
unmentionable	unmistakable
unmixable	unmovable
unnoticeable	unobjectionable
unobservable	unobtainable
unpalatable	unpardonable
unplayable	unpredictable

unprintable	unprofitable
unpronounceable	unquantifiable
unquenchable	unquestionable
unreachable	unreadable
unrealisable	unreasonable
unrecognisable	unrecoverable
unredeemable	unreliable
unremarkable	unrepeatable
unrespectable	unsalvageable
unseasonable	unserviceable
unshakable	unsinkable
unsociable	unsolvable
unspeakable	unstable
unstoppable	unsuitable
unsupportable	unsurpassable
unsustainable	untamable
untenable	unthinkable
untouchable	untraceable
untranslatable	unusable
unutterable	unverifiable
unviable	unwarrantable
unworkable	upgradeable
useable	utilisable
valuable	vaporisable
variable	vegetable
venerable	verifiable
veritable	viable

viewable	violable
vulnerable	warrantable
washable	wearable
weighable	willable
winnable	workable
worktable	writable

The Rule Says

- If you remove -able from a word, you are left with a complete word.
- If you remove -ible from a word, you are not left with a complete word.

Is it '-ie-' or '-ei-'?

Often people get confused whether to use -ie- or -ei- in a spelling. There is a simple rule for it.

The Rule Says

I comes before E except after C

- When the sound is a long 'e' (as in *feed*), write 'i' before 'e', except after 'c'. For Example: believe, yield, reprieve. After 'c' reverse the spelling ('ei'). For example: ceiling, perceive, conceit.

The problem with this rule is that it works only when 'ei'/'ie' sounds like the 'ee' in *feet*. If it has any other sound, you should write 'ei' even after letters other than 'c'. For example foreign, vein, freight.

For example:

- achieve
- believe
- brief
- chief
- friend
- grief

- hygiene
- pierce
- thief
- patience
- priest

Except in case of C

- ceiling
- conceive
- deceive
- receipt
- conceit
- deceit
- perceive
- receive

Exceptions

- When the sound rhymes with 'may', the spelling is -ei-. *For example:* beige, feint, freight, inveigle, neighbour, sleigh, vein, weigh, weight.
- Have a look at a few more common exceptions: either, neither, caffeine, counterfeit, foreign, forfeit, height, leisure, protein, their, weird, seize, seizure.

A Recap for Spelling Plural Nouns

A Common Rule

Most words add 's' to the root forms without any change. However, it should be taken care that -s- is added not just for making plurals, but also for making possessive nouns. These spellings are affected by certain rules.

For example:

- barn > barns
- hand > hands
- kite > kites
- table > tables

Words ending in sh, ch, ss, x and z

Words ending in sh, ch, ss, x and z usually add 'es' to form the plural. Some people describe these as words that 'hiss' at the end.

For example:

- address > addresses
- atlas > atlases
- box > boxes
- brush > brushes
- bush > bushes
- church > churches
- glass > glasses
- sandwich > sandwiches

Words ending in 'y'

If the words ends in a consonant and y, change the y to and add 'es'.

For example:

- bully > bullies
- canary > canaries
- fly > flies
- party > parties
- pony > ponies

If the word has a **vowel** before the final y, then simply add an 's'. For example:

- day > days
- survey > surveys
- toy > toys
- donkey > donkeys
- Sunday > Sundays

Some more Rules

Some words ending in 'f' change the 'f' to 'v' and add 'es'.

For example:

- calf > calves
- elf > elves
- self > selves
- wolf > wolves

Some singular words have different words for their plural form.

For example:

- goose > geese
- man > men
- mouse > mice
- woman > women

CHAPTER 3

Word Families

Word families are groups of words that have a common feature or pattern. They have some of the same combinations of letters in them and a similar sound. *For example:* at, cat, hat and fat are a family of words with the 'at' sound and letter combination in common.

According to one classification, the 37 most common word families in English are: ack, ain, ake, ale, all, ame, an, ank, ap, ash, at, ate, aw, ay, eat, ell, est, ice, ick, ide, ight, ill, in, ine, ing, ink, ip, it, ock, oke, op, ore, ot, uck ,ug, ump and unk.

Common Word Families and Words in them

- **ack:** attack, back, black, crack, Jack, knack, lack, pack, quack, rack, sack, snack, stack, tack, track, whack
- **ad:** ad, bad, dad, had, lad, mad, pad, sad
- **ail:** ail, fail, hail, jail, mail, nail, pail, rail, sail, snail, tail, wail
- **ain:** brain, gain, main, pain, plain, rain, Spain, train
- **ake:** bake, brake, cake, flake, lake, make, rake, stake, take, wake
- **ale:** bale, dale, gale, male, pale, sale, stale, tale
- **all :** ball, call, fall, hall, mall, stall, tall, wall
- **am:** dam, ham, jam, ram, Sam, slam, wham

- **ame**: came, game, fame, name, same, shame, tame
- **an**: an, ban, bran, can, clan, Dan, fan, flan, Fran, ran, span, Stan, tan
- **ank**: bank, blank, crank, plank, prank, rank, sank, tank
- **ap**: cap, clap, flap, gap, lap, map, nap, rap, sap, tap
- **ash**: ash, bash, cash, dash, gash, hash, lash, mash, rash, sash
- **at**: at, bat, brat, cat, chat, fat, flat, hat, mat, pat, rat, sat, sprat, tat, that, vat
- **ate**: ate, crate, date, fate, grate, mate, plate, state
- **aw**: claw, flaw, gnaw, jaw, law, paw, raw, saw, slaw, straw
- **ay**: away, bray, bay, clay, day, gray, hay, lay, may, pay, play, ray, say, spray, stay, sway, tray, way
- **eat**: beat, eat, feat, heat, meat, neat, seat, wheat
- **eel**: eel, feel, heel, peel, wheel
- **eep**: beep, deep, jeep, keep, peep, sheep, sleep, steep, weep
- **eet**: feet, fleet, greet, meet, sleet, sweet
- **ell**: bell, cell, dell, dwell, fell, sell, smell, spell, swell, tell, well
- **en**: Ben, den, fen, gentlemen, hen, men, pen, ten, wren
- **ent**: bent, cent, dent, lent, rent, sent, tent, vent, went
- **est**: best, jest, nest, pest, quest, rest, test, vest, west
- **ice**: ice, dice, nice, mice, rice, slice
- **ick**: kick, lick, nick, pick, quick, Rick, sick, slick, stick, thick, tick, trick, wick
- **ide**: bride, hide, pride, ride, side, slide, tide, wide
- **ife**: knife, life, wife, strife
- **ight**: bright, delight, fight, flight, fright, light, might, night, right, sight, slight, tight, tonight

- **ile**: file, mile, Nile, pile, rile, smile, stile, tile, vile, while
- **ill**: bill, hill, ill, Jill, pill, sill, still, till, will
- **in**: bin, din, grin, in, kin, pin, shin, spin, thin, tin, win
- **ine**: dine, fine, line, mine, nine, pine, swine, tine, vine
- **ing**: bring, cling, fling, king, ping, ring, sing, sling, spring, sting, string, swing, thing, wing, zing
- **ink**: blink, brink, ink, link, mink, pink, rink, sink, think, wink
- **ip**: grip, hip, lip, nip, ship, sip, slip, tip, trip, whip
- **it**: bit, fit, grit, hit, it, kit, lit, pit, quit, sit, spit, twit, wit
- **oat**: boat, coat, float, gloat, goat, oat, throat
- **ock**: block, clock, cock, dock, flock, frock, lock, mock, rock, sock, stock
- **og**: bog, cog, clog, dog, fog, frog, hog, jog, log, slog
- **oil**: boil, broil, coil, foil, oil, soil, spoil, toil
- **oke**: awoke, bloke, broke, joke, poke, spoke, stroke, woke
- **oo**: boo, goo, moo, shoo, too, zoo
- **ood**: good, hood, stood, wood
- **oof**: goof, proof, roof, spoof
- **ook**: book, brook, cook, crook, hook, look, nook, shook, took
- **oom**: bloom, boom, broom, doom, gloom, loom, room, zoom
- **ood**: brood, food, mood
- **ool**: cool, pool, spool, stool, tool
- **oon**: goon, moon, noon, soon, spoon
- **oop**: droop, hoop, loop, scoop, snoop, troop
- **oot (long oo sound)**: boot, hoot, scoot, shoot
- **oot (short oo sound)**: foot, soot

- **op**: bop, cop, crop, drop, flop, mop, pop, stop, top
- **ore**: bore, core, chore, lore, more, ore, pore, sore, store, tore, wore
- **orn**: corn, morn, scorn, thorn
- **ot**: apricot, blot, cot, dot, not, plot, pot, shot, spot, tot
- **ought**: ought, bought, fought, sought, brought, thought
- **ould**: could, should, would
- **ouse**: douse, house, louse, mouse, spouse
- **out**: about, out, pout, shout, spout, stout
- **ow (as sounding in cow)**: bow, cow, how, now, sow, vow, wow, plow, chow
- **ow (as sounding in low)**: bow, blow, crow, flow, glow, grow, low, mow, row, show, slow, snow, sow, stow, throw, tow

This method is an effective way to study how words are spelled. Use this method to study as many words as possible.

CHAPTER 4

Roots

A *root* is the basic element of a word. It is the foundation on which the meaning of a word is built. There are several roots that are real words in their own right, like *graph* means a diagram and *teach* means giving lesson. Such roots can have other elements as well, though they don't need such elements to be complete. Most roots, however, do need other elements. For example, the roots *archy* (government) and *dox* (opinion or belief) need to be combined with other word elements, like prefixes, suffixes, or even other roots, to form complete words. For example:

- Prefix *ortho* (meaning right or true) and root *dox* (meaning opinion or belief) combine to form the word – *Orthodox* (meaning believing what is commonly accepted as true).
- Again, root *-archy* (meaning government), prefix *an* - (meaning against)and the suffix *-ist* (meaning one who) combine to form the word *anarchist* (meaning one who is against archy).
- Prefix *dy-* (meaning two) and root *-archy* (meaning government) give the word *diarchy* (meaning government with two rulers).

In order to use roots to uncover a word's meaning, you need to know a few things about how roots work. Some roots form whole words by themselves. For example: *vent* means 'an opening to allow air to enter' and *audio* means 'sound'. Although these roots form words in themselves, you can also combine them with other word elements (like prefixes and suffixes) to make new words. Look at the following examples:

- **Root:** Arbor

  Word Element: Eal

  New Word: Arboreal (ar-bor-ee-al)

  Part of Speech: Adjective

  Meaning: Of or relating to trees
- **Root:** Vent

  Word Element: Ilate

  New Word: Ventilate (vent-il-ate)

  Part of Speech: Verb

  Meaning: To expose to air
- **Root:** Audio

  Word Element: Ible

  New Word: Audible (aw-di-ble)

  Part of Speech: Adjective

  Meaning: Able to be heard

Some roots must be combined with other word elements to form words. For example:

- **Root:** Capit

  Meaning: Head

  Word Element: Al

  New Word: Capital (kap-ih-tul)

  Part of Speech: Adjective

  New Word's Meaning: Most important
- **Root:** Carn

  Meaning: Flesh

  Word Element: Age

New Word: Carnage (kar-nij)

Part of Speech: Noun

New Word's Meaning: Slaughter

- **Root:** Chrono

  Meaning: Time

  Word Element: Logy

  New Word: Chronology (krah-nahl-ih-jee)

  Part of Speech: Noun

  New Word's Meaning: Timeline

Prefixes and suffixes alter or refine a word's meaning. For example, the word *audible* means 'able to be heard.' With the prefix *in-*, the word becomes *inaudible,* which means 'unable to be heard.'

A word can contain more than one root. For example, the word *matrilineal* contains the roots *matri* (mother) and *lineal* (line). *Matrilineal,* therefore, means 'determining descent through the female line.' Whenever you come upon an unfamiliar word, first check to see if you recognise its root. Even if you can't define a word exactly, recognising the root gives you a general idea of the word's meaning. For example, if you read the word *geocentric*, knowing that the root *geo* means 'earth' helps you figure out that *geocentric* has to do with the center ('centric') of the earth, or earth as the center.

Latin Roots

Here is a list of Latin roots with their meanings and examples.

Latin Root	Meaning	English Word(s)
act	act or do	Actual
ami	like or love	Amiable
aqua	water	Aquatic, Aqueduct

audio	hear	Audience, Audible
cad	fall	Cadence
ced	go	Intercede
centurn	a hundred	Century, Centipede, Centimetre, Cent
cept	take, hold	Intercept
cid	kill or cut	Genocide
clud	shut or close	Occlude
cred	believe	Incredulous
cur	run	Incur
dict	tell	Edict
duct	lead	Induct
duo	two	Dual, Duet
fact	make or do	Benefactor
fer	bear or carry	Confer
flect	flex or bend	Genuflect
gress	step or go forward	Egress
here	stick or adhere	Inherent
ject	throw	Eject
junct	join	Conjunction
leg	read or choose	Illegible
loqu	talk or speak	Loquacity
luna	moon	Lunar, Lunatic
magnus	great	Magnify, Magnificent, Magnitude
malus	bad	Maltreat, Malaria
mare	sea	Marine, Submarine
mikros	small	Microscope, Micro organism

mit	send	Transmit
mov	move	Immovable
ped	foot	Centipede
pedis	foot	Pedestrian, Pedal
pel	drive	Impel
pend	hang	Pendulum
pon	put	Respond
port	carry	Transport
press	press or hold	Impress
rupt	break	Disrupt
scrib	write	Describe
sect	cut	Intersect
sent	feel	Sentient
Sentio	I feel	Sentiment, Sentimental
sequ	follow	Sequence
spect	look	Introspection
sta	stand	Station
tact	touch	Tactile
termin	end	Determine
Terra	the earth	Territory, Terrier
tract	draw, pull	Tractor
unus	one	Unicycle, Unicorn
vent	come	Invent
vert	turn	Convert
vict	conquer	Evict
vid	see	Video
voc	call	Vocalise
volv	roll or turn	Evolve

Greek Roots

The following table shows a list of Greek roots along with their meanings and examples:

Greek Root	Meaning	English Word(s)
aster -	a star	Astrology, Asterisk
bote-	herb or plant	Botany, Botanist
chrono-	time	Chronology, Chronometer
dend-	tree	Dendrite, Philodendron
-hemia	blood	Polycythemia
hydro -	water	Hydrant, Hydrofoil, Hydrogen
-iasis	a pathological condition	Hypochondriasis, Psoriasis
lithy-	stone	Lithoglyph, Lithography
metron -	measure	Barometer, Thermometer
okto -	eight	Octopus, Octagon
pachy	thick	Pachycephalic, Pachyderm
rrhage-	to burst forth	Haemorrhage, Menorrhagia
tele -	far	Telescope, Telephone
thermos -	hot	Thermometer, Thermostat

Greek Affixes

The following table shows a list of Greek affixes that are often used with roots.

Greek Affix	Meaning	English Word
anthropo	man	Anthropologist
anti	against	Antihistamine
astro	star	Astrology
auto	self	Automobile
biblio	book	Bibliography

bio	life	Biosphere
chrom	colour	Monochromatic
chron	time	Chronology
cosmo	world	Microcosm
cracy	government	Autocracy
dem	people	Demographic
eu	well or good	Euphemism
geo	earth	Geography
graph	write	Autograph
hydro	water	Hydrophobia
hyper	over	Hyperactive
hypo	under	Hypodermic
log	speech or word	Syllogism
logy	science or study	Meteorology
meta	beyond	Metaphysics
meter	measure	Hygrometer
micro	small	Microorganism
mis	hate, wrong	Misogyny
mono	one	Monosyllable
onym	name	Synonym
pan	all	Pantheism
path	feeling	Sympathy
peri	around	Peripatetic
phil	love	Anglophile
phob	fear	Agoraphobia
phon	sound	Megaphone
poly	many	Polyphony
pseudo	false	Pseudonym
psych	mind	Psychology

scop	see	Oscilloscope
soph	wisdom	Sophomore
syn	together	Synchronise
tele	at a distance	Telemetry

Prefixes

In English, prefixes convey meanings. Largely derived from Latin, these elements carry into English their Latin origins. Again, the regularity of these structural or meaningful elements makes the spelling of many words highly predictable.

Have a look at some common prefixes:

Prefix	Meaning	Word(s)
a-, an-	not or without	Amoral, Anesthetic, Apolitical, Asocial
ab-	away from	Abduction, Abstain, Abnormal
ad-	to or toward	Adjoin, Adjacent (lying near to)
ambi-	both	Ambidextrous, Ambivalent
ana-	up, back or again	Analogy, Anatomy, Anagram
anti-	against	Antipathy, Antiwar, Antisocial
apo-	from or away from	Apology, Apologise
auto-	self	Autobiography, Automobile, Autocracy, Automaton
bene-	good	Benediction, Benevolent, Benefactor
cata-, cat-	down or against	Catastrophe (a turning down)
centro, centri-	around, center	Concentric, Centrifugal

circum-	around	Circumlocution Circumference, Circumvent
com-	with or together	Communal, Community
con-	with or together	Connect, Confide, Conspire
contra-	against	Contradict, Contravene
de-	down or away	Descend, Deject (cast down)
dia-, di-	through or across	Diameter, Division
dis-	apart or not	Disengage, Discord, Discomfort
dys-	ill, difficult or bad	Dysfunctional, Dysentery
e-	out of or from	Elect (choose out of), Eject (throw out)
ecto-	on the outside	Ectoderm (outer skin)
en- or em-	in	Empathy (feeling in)
endo-	within or inside	Endoscope (instrument for observing inside)
epi-	upon	Epitaph, Epidermis, Epicenter
eso-	inward or within	Esoteric (more inward), Esophagus
eu-	well or good	Euthanasia (good death)
ex-	out of or from	Exhume, Exhale, Exodus
hetero-	other or different	Heterosexual, Heterodoxy, Heterodox, Heterogeneous
homo-	same	Homosexual, Homogeneous, Homogenised
hyper-	over	Hypertension, Hypersensitive, Hyperactivity

hypo-	under	Hypotension, Hypodermic
il-	not	Illegitimate, Illicit, Illegal, Illegible
im-	not	Imperfect, Impolite, Impossible
im-	into	Imbibe (drink in, take in)
in-	not	Indiscreet, Invisible
in-	into	Incorporate (take into the body)
inter-	between	Intervene (come between), Interstate
intra-	within	Intrastate, Intramural
ir-	not	Irregular, Irrational, Irredeemable
macro-	large	Macrocosm, Macroeconomics
mal, male-	bad or evil	Malediction, Malevolent, Malnutrition
meta-	beyond	Metaphysical
micro-	small	Microscope, Microcosm, Microeconomics
mono-	one or single	Monologue, Monotheism, Monarchy, Monogamy
neo-	new or recent	Neologism, Neo-liberal, Neonatology, Neolithic
ob-	against	Object, Obstruct (build against)
palin-, pali-	back or again	Palindrome
pan-	all or every	Pantheism, panorama, Pandemic
para-	false	Paramilitary, Paralegal, Parachute

per-	through	Percolate (flow through), Perforate (punch through)
peri-	around	Perimeter, Periscope
phil-, philo-	like or lover of	Philosophy, Francophile, Bibliophile, Philanthropy
poly-	many or several	Polygon, Polygamy, Polytechnic, Polytheism
post-	after	Postgraduate, Posthumous Postpone
pre-	before	Precede, Predict (tell before)
pro-	for or forward	Promote, Project
pros-	toward or in front	Prospect (view in front or something coming up)
proto-	first	Prototype, Protoplasm, Protobiology
pseudo	false	Pseudonym, Pseudoscience
re-	again or back	Repeat, Recede, Regress (step back)
retro-	back	Retrogression, Retroactive
se-	away from	Seduce (lead away), Secede
sub-	under	Submarine, Subject, Subhuman, Subterranean
sur- or super-	over or above	Superhuman, Superego, Superintend, Surpass
syn-, sym-, syl- or sys-	with or together	Symphony, Synonym, System, Syllable
tele-	distant or far off	Telephone, Telepathy, Television, Telegram
trans-	across	Transient, Transatlantic, Transport (carry across)

English Suffixes

Suffixes in English serve two functions: they indicate inflection (tense, number, comparison etc.), and they indicate parts of speech (noun, verb, adjective, adverb etc.). The regularity of these structural elements make the spelling of these parts of words predictable. The meaning these elements convey is grammatical function.

Inflectional Suffixes

Tense	Number	Comparison
-ing	-s	-er
-ed	-es	-est
	-n	

Derivational Suffixes

Noun	Verb	Adjective	Adverb
-tion	-ise	-ous	-ly
-ment	-ate	-able	- ally
-ity	-fy	-ible	
-sion	-en	-ive	
-ness	-ant	-ary	
-ance	-ent		
-ence	-al		
-ency	-ful		
-ture	-less		
-al	-ic		
-y	-ish		
-ist	-ine		
-ory			
-ing			
-cy			

Have a look at some common suffixes.

Suffix	Meaning	Word(s)
-agog or -agogue	leader	Demagogue, Pedagogue
-cide	kill(ing)	Patricide, Infanticide, Herbicide, Suicide

-ectomy	cutting	Appendectomy, Splenectomy
-ia or -y	act or state	Amnesia, Mania, Democracy, Anarchy
-ic, -tic, -ical or ac	having to do with	Anthropomorphic, Dramatic, Biblical, Cardiac
-ics	things having to do with	Optics, Physics
-isk or -iscus	small	Asterisk (a little star)
-ism	the belief in	Pacifism, Terrorism, Socialism, Communism
-ist	one who believes in	Pacifist, Terrorist, Socialist, Communist
-ite	one connected with	Meteorite, Polite, Cosmopolite
-logy	study field of	Biology, Geology, Etymology, Cardiology
-oid	resembling or like-shaped	Asteroid, Spheroid
-or, -er	one who takes part in	Doctor, Actor, Teacher, Driver
-phobia	exaggerated fear	Photophobia, Claustrophobia, Agoraphobia
-sis	act, state or condition of	Analysis

Roots to Grow Words

Knowing how words are created gives you the key to figuring out the meaning of new words. When you can put together the meaning of a root with the meaning of a prefix and/or a suffix, you can unlock the definitions of words in a snap. This also helps in learning spelling words.

Adding prefixes and suffixes

A *prefix* is a letter or group of letters attached to the beginning of a word that changes the word's meaning. A *suffix* performs the same function at the end of a word.

Examples of adding a prefix to a root:

- *de* + hydrate = dehydrate (to remove the water or moisture from)
- *anti* + depressant = antidepressant (something that combats depression)

Examples of adding a suffix to a root:

- zoo + *ology* = zoology (the study of animals)
- bronch + *itis* = bronchitis (inflammation of the bronchial tubes)

You can figure out a word's meaning simply by recognising its root and prefix. Have a look at some more examples of how the combination of prefixes, roots, and suffixes work together to form words.

Prefix	+Root	+ Suffix	=	Word	Part of Speech	Meaning
ab	+duct	+ ed	=	Abducted	Verb	Kidnapped
de	+ter	+ ent	=	Deterrent	Adjective	Obstruction
dis	+ pell	+ ed	=	Dispelled	Verb	Scattered
im	+ peril	+ ed	=	Imperilled	Verb	Put in danger
in	+ cred	+ ible	=	Incredible	Adjective	Unbelievable
re	+ puls	+ ion	=	Repulsion	Noun	Strong dislike
re	+ ferr	+ al	=	Referral	Noun	Connection
re	+ tract	+ able	=	Retractable	Adjective	Able to be drawn back

Compound Words

Once you are comfortable with roots and the spellings you can learn through them, you can move forward with compound words to become comfortable with rather difficult words. Compound words are made when two words are joined to form a new word. Have a look at a few examples of compound words.

Root Word 1	Root Word 2	Compound Word
Bed	Rock	Bedrock
Brow	Lid	Brow-lid
Bud	Pot	Budpot
Copper	Ware	Copperware
Eye	Drop	Eyedrop
Finger	Print	Fingerprint
Flower	Pot	Flowerpot
Hand	Bag	Handbag
Head	Dress	Headdress
Lady	Bug	Ladybug
News	Stand	Newsstand
Paper	Clip	Paperclip
Penny	Royal	Pennyroyal
Pig	Tail	Pigtail
Print	Nail	Printnail
Sand	Paper	Sandpaper
Shake	Out	Shakeout
Storm	Bound	Stormbound
Thumb	Tack	Thumbtack
Time	Piece	Timepiece

In English, words, particularly adjectives and nouns, are combined into compound structures in a variety of ways. After they are formed once sometimes they metamorphose over time. A common pattern is that two words — fire fly, say — will be joined by a hyphen for a time (fire-fly). Later, it will be joined into one word — firefly.

There are three forms of compound words:

- the **closed form**, in which the words are joined together, such as firefly, softball, childlike, redhead, keyboard, makeup, notebook;
- the **hyphenated form**, such as daughter-in-law, master-at-arms, over-the-counter, six-pack, six-year-old, mass-produced; and
- the **open form**, such as post office, real estate, middle class, full moon, half sister, attorney general.

Modifying compounds are often hyphenated to avoid confusion. When compounded modifiers precede a noun, they are often hyphenated, like *part-time teacher, fifty-yard-wide field, fire-resistant curtains, high-speed chase*. When those same modifying words come after the noun, however, they are not hyphenated, like *a field fifty yards wide, curtains that are fire resistant*, etc. The *second-rate* opera company gave a performance that was *first rate*.

Comparative and superlative forms of adjectives are hyphenated when compounded with other modifiers, like *the highest-priced car*, *the shorter-term loan* etc.. But, this is not always the case: *the most talented youngster*. Adverbs, words ending in -*ly*, are not hyphenated when compounded with other modifiers like a *highly rated bank, a partially refunded ticket, publicly held securities* etc.

Sometimes hyphenated modifiers lose their hyphens when they become compound nouns.

For example:

- A clear *decision-making* process was evident in his *decision making*.

- The *bluish grey* was slowly disappearing from the *bluish-grey* sky.

This is not always so, however: the *high-rise apartment* building is also known as a *high-rise.*

When modifying a person with his or her age, the compounded phrase is hyphenated, like *my six-year-old son*. However, when the age comes after the person, we don't use a hyphen. For example, my son is *six years old*. He is, however, *a six-year-old*.

Plurals and Possessives

Most dictionaries give different spellings of compound plurals. For example, *When you have more than one truck filled with sand, do you have several truckfuls or trucksful?* The dictionary will give you both, with the first spelling usually preferred. For hyphenated forms, the pluralising *-s* is usually attached to the element that is actually being pluralised, like *daughters-in-law, half-moons, mayors-elect*.

As a general rule, the plural form of an element in a hierarchical term belongs to the base element in the term, regardless of the base element's placement.

For example:

- colonel **generals**
- deputy assistant **secretaries** of state
- deputy **librarians**
- first **sergeants**
- lieutenant **colonels**
- lieutenant **generals**
- **sergeants** first class
- **sergeants** major

The possessive of a hyphenated compound is created by attaching an apostrophe -s to the end of the compound itself, like ***daughter-in-law's car***, ***friend of mine's car***. In case of confusion, create the possessive of pluralised and compounded forms, avoid the apostrophe -*s* form and use an 'of' phrase (the 'post genitive') instead, like the meeting of the daughters-in-law, the schedule of half-moons. Otherwise, the possessive form becomes downright weird, like daughters-in-law's meeting, friends of mine's cars, etc.

CHAPTER 5

American and British Spellings

There are differences in the spelling and words used by British and those used by Americans. So, a spelling that might be right in an American book might not really be in a British one.

Have a look at prominent differences in British and American spellings:

American	British	Difference
-ize	-ise	British tend to prefer -ise to -ize. However -ize is becoming more acceptable in Britain.
-or	-our	British use -our at the end of colour, humour, favour, and a few others. But words which indicate a person who does something always end with -or, for example: actor, survivor, curator, etc.
-er	-re	British use -re at the end of words such as centre, metre, theatre, etc.

Common Spelling Differences

American Spelling	British Spelling	American Spelling	British Spelling
airplane	aeroplane	flotation	floatation

esthetics	aesthetics	inquire	enquire
analyze	analyse	gram	gramme
archeology	archaeology	honor	honour
ax	axe	homo~	haemo~
bail out	bale out	karat	carat
baloney	boloney	labor	labour
B.S.	B.Sc.	licorice	liquorice
cesarean	caesarean	maneuver	manoeuvre
caldron	cauldron	marvelous	marvellous
check	cheque	medieval	medieval
checker	chequer	mold	mould
chili	chilli	mustache	moustache
citrus	citrous	monolog	monologue
color	colour	M.S.	M.Sc.
connection	connexion	neighbor	neighbour
counselor	counsellor	offense	offence
defense	defence	organize	organise
diarrhea	diarrhoea	pajamas	pyjamas
dialog	dialogue	paralyze	paralyse
donut	doughnut	parlor	parlour
draftman	draughtsman	practice	practise
drafty	draughty	program	programme
encyclopedia	encyclopaedia	savor	savour
endeavor	endeavour	skeptical	sceptical
estrogen	oestrogen	story (Building)	storey
favor	favour	travelers	travellers
fetus	foetus	tire	tyre
flavor	flavour		

Common Word Differences

Apart from spelling, these are some of the differences in vocabulary between British and American English.

British word	American word	British word	American word
angry/cross	mad	barrister	attorney
autumn	fall	biscuit	cookie
block of flats	apartment or building	bonnet (of a car)	hood (of a car)
boot (of a car)	truck (of a car)	aubergine	egg plant
caravan	trailer or mobile home	beet root	beet
chemist (shop)	drug store	chest of drawers	bureau
chips	French fries	chocolate bar	candy bar
crisps	potato chips	crossroads	intersection
the cinema	the movies	clothes peg	clothes pin
film	movies	estate agent	realtor
cupboard	closet	cutlery	silverware
diversion	detour	motor	engine
drawing pin	thumb tack or push pin	flat	apartment
dustbin	trash can/ garbage can	flyover	overpass
gear lever	gear shift	girl guide	girl scout
ground floor	first floor	handbag	purse
hold-all	bag	sweets	candy bar
tap (indoor)	faucet	taxi	cab or taxi
tap (outdoor)	spigot	tea towel	dish towel
telly	TV	timetable	schedule

third party insurance	liability insurance	tin	can
toll motorway	turnpike	torch	flash light
trousers	pants	pants	underwear
tube (train)	subway	aerial	antenna
underground (train)	subway	call box	pay phone
bank holiday	legal or public holiday	Christian name	first name
anti clockwise	counter clockwise	dinner jacket	tuxedo
current account	checking account	engaged (phone)	busy (phone)
fortnight	two weeks	lift	elevator
interval	intermission	maths	math
milometer	odometer	mudguard	fender
pavement	sidewalk	petrol	gas/gasoline
post box	mail box	reverse change	collect call
round about	traffic circle	cooker	stove
lorry	truck	duvet	comforter
comforter (baby)	pacifier (baby)	nappy	diaper
noughts and crosses	tick tack toe		

CHAPTER 6

Confusing Words

Many words sound alike but mean different things when put into writing. Due to their sound, people often get confused regarding their use and spelling. Here is a comprehensive list of such words and their usage to help you avoid errors while using them:

A

- **allot** (give out or distribute)

  Usage: We will **allot** the prizes on the decided date.

  alot - There is no such word as alot.

  a lot (many; much)

  Usage: A lot of people are doing business in the town.

  Usage: Some women worry **a lot** about their weight.

- **allowed** (permitted)

  Usage: No one under 17 was **allowed.**

  aloud (audibly)

  Usage: He read the book **aloud.**

- **allusion** (indirect or casual mention)

  Usage: No one made any **allusion** to the scandal.

  illusion (presentation of a false or misleading idea)

  Usage: The magician gave the **illusion** of sawing the child in half.

delusion (mistaken belief while in a confused state of mind)

Usage: He was under the **delusion** that he could fly.

elusion (evasion or clever escape)

Usage: The cops celebrated their **elusion** of the robbers a little too soon.

- **altar** (worship table)

  Usage: The priest approached the **altar.**

  alter (change)

  Usage: It is hard to **alter** a determined man's plans.

- **alternate** (occurring by turns)

  Usage: She works on **alternate** weekends.

  alternative (providing or expressing a choice)

  Usage: An **alternative** to designing your own gown is hiring a designer.

- **amend** (modify or revise)

  Usage: It's time to **amend** our by-laws.

  emend (alter or correct in the text of a written work)

  Usage: The publishers hurried to **emend** the book before the next edition.

- **among** (in the midst of three or more)

  Usage: The four older children decided **among** themselves to surprise their parents with breakfast in bed.

  between (in the midst of two)

  Usage: The two younger boys decided **between** themselves to clean the kitchen.

- **ante-** (prefix meaning before)

  Usage: The abbreviation A.M. stands for **ante** meridian, meaning before noon.

  anti- (prefix meaning against)

Usage: The **anti-**American protesters marched in the capital city.

- **antecedence** (act of going before in time)

  Usage: The **antecedence** of parents to their own children is a fact of life.

  antecedents (individuals who have gone before)

  Usage: His **antecedents** left him a fortune, but he wasted most of it.

- **any one** (whichever unit)

  Usage: You can have **any one** of these apples.

- **anyone** (any person whatever)

  Usage: "**Anyone** having information about the whereabouts of the suspect, please come forward," requested the cop.

- **any way** (by a choice of methods)

  Usage: She was determined to succeed **any way** she could.

  anyway (in any case or nevertheless)

  Usage: Rohan didn't like the movie **anyway.**

- **apportion** (divide up and distribute by shares)

  Usage: "I want to **apportion** the money among all the children," the man announced.

  portion (a limited amount of something)

  Usage: He didn't eat his **portion** of ice-cream.

  proportion (ratio of one thing to another)

  Usage: The **proportion** of women to men using the Internet is increasing.

- **appraise** (judge the value of)

  Usage: A businessman takes many factors into account in order to appraise his product.

- **apprise** (to inform or notify)

  Usage: "Please **apprise** the class of the changes," said the teacher.

- **arc** (a curved line)

  Usage: A rainbow is an **arc.**

- **ark** (a large, flat-bottomed boat)

  Usage: They loaded the grain on the **ark** and floated it down the river.

- **are** (form of 'to be')

  Usage: "What **are** you going to do now?" he asked.

  hour (sixty minutes)

  Usage: "It seemed like I waited an **hour,** but it was only twenty minutes," he said.

  our (belonging to us)

  Usage: "Please visit **our** house next week," said the Aroras.

- **area** (region)

  Usage: "What **area** of the country are you from?" asked the man.

  aria (an elaborate song for one voice)

  Usage: When the soprano finished the **aria**, the audience clapped.

- **arrears** (unpaid debts)

  Usage: "We cannot extend you any credit because your account is already in **arrears,"** the clerk said.

  arraign (call into court)

  Usage: The suspect will be **arraigned** next week.

  arrange (put into order)

  Usage: It is very important how you **arrange** the articles in your store.

- **assay** (chemical analysis)

  Usage: The **assay** office will test your ore to see how much gold it contains.

  essay (a short composition expressing author's opinions)

  Usage: Students applying for a scholarship often have to write an **essay.**

- **assistance** (help)

  Usage: Any **assistance** you can give me will be welcome.

  assistants (helpers)

  Usage: The teacher's two **assistants** handed out the tests.

- **assure** (declare positively)

  Usage: "I **assure** you that the work will be finished by next Tuesday," he said.

  ensure (make sure)

  Usage: Order today to **ensure** the delivery of the product.

  insure (cover by insurance)

  Usage: The company **insures** the data on the hard disk as well as the computer itself.

- **at present** (right now)

  Usage: Ratan is designing a small-business website **at present.**

  presently (in a little while or shortly)

  Usage: "Mr. Kothari will be down to see you **presently,**" the servant said.

- **ate** (past tense of eat)

  Usage: We **ate** at that new restaurant last week.

  eight (the number after seven)

  Usage: Breakfast will be at **eight** in the morning.

- **attendance** (being present)

  Usage: Part of your grade is based on **attendance.**

  attendants (workers)

  Usage: The flight **attendants** served the dinner.

- **autobiography** (one's own life story)

  Usage: I am writing my **autobiography.**

  bibliography (list of books about a subject)

  Usage: Please include a **bibliography** with your research report.

  biography (a person's life story)

  Usage: She is writing a **biography** of the club president.

B

- **bail** (security given for release from jail)

  Usage: The **bail** was granted as per orders from the court.

  bale (a large bundle)

  Usage: The hay was collected together and compressed into a **bale.**

- **bare** (exposed to view)

  Usage: The **bare** branches of the trees made lacy patterns against the winter sky.

  bear (carry or transport; tolerate, stand or endure; a large mammal)

  Usage: I **bear** a gift for you.

  Usage: I can't **bear** to hear another word.

  Usage: At the zoo the kids saw a **bear.**

- **base** (the bottom part which supports that above it)

  Usage: The group camped overnight at the **base** of the mountain.

bass (deep or low in sound)

Usage: "You sing the high notes, and I'll sing the **bass,"** she said.

- **bases** (plural of base; plural of basis)

Usage: The army is closing down its **bases** in that country.

Usage: The **bases** of all his theories were flawed.

basis (fundamental principal)

Usage: Your accusation has no **basis** in fact.

- **bazaar** (marketplace)

Usage: The charity held a fund-raising **bazaar**.

- **bizarre** (very odd)

Usage: Her outfit was too **bizarre** for the workplace.

- **beat** (strike repeatedly; defeat)

Usage: Percussion bands **beat** their drums at an unbelievable tempo.

Usage: Your team will never **beat** the champions.

beet (root vegetable)

Usage: The common red **beet** can be cooked and eaten.

- **berry** (small, pulpy fruit with many seeds)

Usage: The kid loves **berry** pie.

bury (put in the ground and cover)

Usage: If we **bury** the treasure no one will find it.

- **berth** (a resting place)

Usage: "When we go on the train, which **berth** do you want, upper or lower?" the mother asked her son.

birth (being born)

Usage: The **birth** of the first child is a happy occasion for parents.

- **beside** (by the side of)

  Usage: Sit down **beside** the fire and get warm.

  besides (moreover or else)

  Usage: She didn't want to go to the party; **besides,** she wasn't really wanted there.

- **billed** (sent a statement of money owed)

  Usage: "Would you like to pay cash now or be **billed**?" the salesman asked.

  build (construct or assemble)

  Usage: You can **build** good credit by paying bills on time.

- **blew** (sent forth a current of air)

  Usage: The wind **blew** across the desert.

  blue (a colour; depressed feeling)

  Usage: The editor marked corrections with a **blue** pen.

  Usage: Her **blue** mood upset everyone.

- **bloc** (group with a shared purpose)

  Usage: The measure was opposed by the farm **bloc.**

  block (a chunk; hinder)

  Usage: He is going to carve a rose from that **block** of wood.

  Usage: The police lined up the cars to **block** the robbers' path.

- **board** (piece of wood; council)

  Usage: The diver hit his head on the **board.**

  Usage: "I'll make your suggestion to the **board** of trustees," said the manager.

  bored (tired of the monotony)

  Usage: After ten speeches, the audience got **bored** because every speaker said the same thing.

- **boarder** (a lodger who receives meals regularly at a fixed price)

  Usage: "To earn extra money, we took in a **boarder,**" the woman revealed.

  border (boundary)

  Usage: Be sure to have your passport when you cross the **border.**

- **bolder** (more daring)

  Usage: If you want to be noticed, perhaps you need to be a little **bolder.**

  boulder (a large rock)

  Usage: The road was blocked by a **boulder.**

- **born** (brought into existence)

  Usage: A new nation was **born** from the ashes of the defeated one.

  borne (carried; tolerated)

  Usage: All their belongings were **borne** on their shoulders.

  Usage: Unjustified outbursts should not be **borne.**

- **boy** (male child)

  Usage: "Is the new baby a **boy** or a girl?" asked the man.

  buoy (a floating marker in the water)

  Usage: When they saw the **buoy,** they knew they were entering the channel.

- **brake** (device that helps you stop)

  Usage: When the driver saw the cow on the road, he hit the **brake.**

  break (rupture, fracture or crack)

  Usage: "Don't play ball in the house, because you'll **break** something," said the woman.

- **bread** (food made of grain)

  Usage: They gave homemade soup and fresh **bread** to the guests.

  bred (past tense of breed)

  Usage: Some dogs are **bred** for strength, some for vigil.

- **breadth** (width or broadness)

  Usage: The **breadth** of his knowledge of world history surprised everyone.

  breath (respiration)

  Usage: The doctor asked him to hold his **breath** while taking the X-ray.

  breathe (inhale and exhale)

  Usage: The doctor asked him to **breathe** in fresh air.

- **bridal** (having to do with a marriage ceremony)

  Usage: The **bridal** bouquet was made of daisies and wildflowers.

  bridle (having to do with horseback riding; restrain or control)

  Usage: The **bridle** path was crowded that morning with weekend riders.

  Usage: "I wish I could learn to **bridle** my tongue," the boy said.

- **broach** (introduce)

  Usage: "While the boss was in a good mood, I decided to **broach** the subject of a raise," said the man.

  brooch (ornamental pin)

  Usage: She wore a beautiful diamond **brooch.**

- **bouillon** (clear soup with a strong flavour)

  Usage: For the first course they made beef **bouillon.**

bullion (precious metals, formed into bars)

Usage: The coach was loaded with hundreds of bars of gold **bullion.**

- **buy** (purchase)

Usage: More and more customers are willing to **buy** goods from an online storefront.

by (through the action of)

Usage: The new proposal was presented **by** the manager.

bye (short form of goodbye)

Usage: "**Bye** for now!" said the kind.

C

- **cache** (hidden storage)

Usage: "Lost in the woods, we were happy to find a **cache** of food belonging to some hunters," the boy recalled.

cash (money paid at the time of purchase)

Usage: The employees demanded their salary in **cash.**

- **calendar** (device for showing divisions of time)

Usage: He marked the date of the woman's arrival on the **calendar.**

colander (strainer)

Usage: Use the **colander** to drain the noodles.

- **callous** (unfeeling)

Usage: Drinking and driving shows a **callous** disregard for life.

callus (hard, thickened skin)

Usage: Shweta got a **callus** on her finger from holding the pencil.

- **canvas** (durable cloth made from cotton, linen or hemp)

Usage: The fine painting was oil on **canvas.**

canvass (go around asking)

Usage: "**Canvass** the neighbourhood to see if anyone saw the suspect," said the cop.

- **capital** (city where the seat of government of a state or country is located; upper case letter)

  Usage: Washington, D. C. is the **capital** of the United States of America.

  Usage: Writing in all **capitals** during online chat is considered shouting, and is rude.

  Capitol (building in which the U. S. Congress meets)

  Usage: When the group visited Washington, D. C., they toured the **Capitol.**

- **carton** (lightweight container or box)

  Usage: "Please send me one **carton** of printer cartridges," request the customer.

  cartoon (drawing, often humorous)

  Usage: Garfield is a popular **cartoon** character.

- **casual** (informal)

  Usage: For a picnic in the park, it's best to wear **casual** clothes.

  causal (relating to a cause)

  Usage: The **causal** forces behind many diseases have not been discovered yet.

- **cease** (stop)

  Usage: They **ceased** coming after the incident.

  seize (grab)

  Usage: The guerillas tried to **seize** control of the town.

  siege (prolonged period of trouble or annoyance)

  Usage: Our family has had a **siege** of bad colds this year.

- **cede** (yield)

  Usage: At the end of war the loser has to **cede** the disputed territory to the winner.

  seed (beginning of a new plant)

  Usage: The **seed** of an avocado can be planted in soil or water.

- **ceiling** (upper limit of a room)

  Usage: A light-coloured **ceiling** makes a room look brighter.

  sealing (closing airtight)

  Usage: **Sealing** the containers is important to keep the contents fresh.

- **cell** (small room)

  Usage: She will have to spend two months in a prison **cell** for her crime.

  sell (offer for sale)

  Usage: The man went to the agent to **sell** his house.

- **cellar** (underground room)

  Usage: "In our house, the **cellar** was always damp," recalled the kid.

  seller (one who offers for sale)

  Usage: He is a **seller** of books.

- **census** (population count)

  Usage: The last **census** showed an increase in single-parent families.

  senses (sound mental faculties)

  Usage: "Don't call me until you have come to your **senses,**" the girl shouted.

- **cent** (one-hundredth of a monetary unit)

Usage: In the U.S., a penny is worth one **cent.**

scent (odour)

Usage: The detective smelled the **scent** of almonds.

sent (past tense of send)

Usage: They **sent** a letter at the mentioned address.

- **cents** (plural of cent)

  Usage: His opinion is only worth two **cents.**

  sense (method of perception)

  Usage: Ears provide us with the **sense** of hearing.

- **cereal** (breakfast food prepared from grain)

  Usage: The girl's favourite **cereal** is Grape-Nuts.

- **serial** (arranged in a series)

  Usage: The cops are working to trap that **serial** killer.

- **cession** [act of ceding (surrendering) to another]

  Usage: The treaty included **cession** of all captured territories.

  session (meeting or term)

  Usage: "I will take two classes during the summer **session,**" the professor said.

- **chews** (grinding with teeth)

  Usage: She **chews** her food carefully.

  choose (select)

  Usage: There are many good programmes to **choose** from.

  chose (past tense of choose)

  Usage: They **chose** a girl for their only son.

- **chord** (a combination of musical tones played simultaneously)

  Usage: His symphony is entitled The Lost **Chord.**

cord (small rope)

Usage: "You need to pull the silver **cord** to summon the maid," the servant informed.

- **chute** (slanted shaft from a higher level to a lower one)

  Usage: The gravel came rumbling down the **chute.**

  shoot (to discharge a weapon)

  Usage: The general commanded them to **shoot.**

- **cite** (quote)

  Usage: "Your proposal will be more persuasive if you **cite** results of a recent survey," the manager suggested.

  sight (vision)

  Usage: Our eyes provide us with the sense of **sight.**

  site (exact location)

  Usage: The labour needed material on the construction **site.**

- **cliché** (overused expression)

  Usage: A good business writer tries to avoid using a **cliché.**

  click (make a light, sharp sound)

  Usage: The instructions said to **click** on the left mouse button.

  clique (small, exclusive group of people)

  Usage: "I wasn't invited to join their **clique,**" the boy said.

- **climactic** (having to do with the climax of something)

  Usage: The villain falling off the cliff was the **climactic** scene of the movie.

  climatic (having to do with climate)

  Usage: The **climatic** conditions in the South Pole can be simply described as cold.

- **close** (shut)

  Usage: Please **close** the door when you leave.

  clothes (wearing apparel)

  Usage: Wear your nicest business **clothes** for your interview for that job.

- **cloths** (pieces of fabric)

  Usage: "Use the **cloths** under the sink for dusting," said the woman.

- **coarse** (rough)

  Usage: Their garments were made of a **coarse** cloth.

  course (natural development; a unit of study)

  Usage: The doctor said the disease must run its **course.**

  Usage: She got an A in English **course.**

- **collision** (crash)

  Usage: "Was anyone hurt in the **collision?**" asked the lady.

- **collusion** (conspiracy)

  Usage: The price rise was due to **collusion** among the manufacturers.

- **coma** (unconscious state)

  Usage: The accident victim was in a **coma** for six months.

  comma (punctuation mark)

  Usage: Use a **comma** to show where you would normally pause if you were reading the sentence aloud.

- **command** (give an order)

  Usage: That sounded more like a **command** than a request.

  commend (praise)

  Usage: "I **commend** you for the effort in reading this list," the teacher said.

- **commence** (begin)

  Usage: The office **commences** work at 9 am.

  comments (remarks)

  Usage: I appreciate your **comments** about this list," the teacher said.

- **complement** (that which completes)

  Usage: As an author, he needs input from readers to **complement** his point of view.

  compliment (expression of praise)

  Usage: Sometimes a critical remark is more useful than a **compliment.**

- **comprehensible** (understandable)

  Usage: The instructions were **comprehensible.**

  comprehensive (covering a wide area)

  Usage: In order to graduate, one must take a **comprehensive** examination of the subject.

- **confidant** (someone you tell secrets to)

  Usage: "He was always my best friend and **confidant,"** revealed the girl.

  confident (self-assured)

  Usage: Applicants should be **confident** about themselves.

- **confidentially** (spoken in a private manner)

  Usage: "Confidentially, I am looking for another job," the man said.

- **confidently** (firmly assured)

  Usage: You can **confidently** raise your arms in public if you use a certain brand of deodorant.

- **conscience** (inner sense of right and wrong)

Usage: Wouldn't it bother your **conscience** to lie to your friends?

conscious (aware or awake)

Usage: The patient was **conscious** for an hour and then relapsed into a coma.

- **conservation** (protection from loss or waste)

Usage: The company shows concern about **conservation** of bandwidth by making efficient webpages.

conversation (talk between people)

Usage: "I very much enjoyed our **conversation** yesterday," the boy said.

- **consul** (representative of a foreign government)

Usage: For the next seminar about exporting, they looked for a **consul** from an Eastern European country to be a featured speaker.

council (elected or appointed group of people assembled for governing or advising)

Usage: "We're going to have to take that idea up with the town **council**," the man said.

counsel (give advice or opinion; attorney)

Usage: Volunteers **counsel** the young people.

Usage: He had the contract drawn up on advice of **counsel.**

- **consular** (having to do with the representative of a foreign government)

Usage: Mr. Mehta is the man in charge of **consular** affairs at the Consulate.

councillor (appointed or elected member of a council)

Usage: As **councillor** for this township, he welcomed people's ideas.

counsellor (advisor)

Usage: You need a letter from your guidance **counsellor** for your scholarship application.

- **continual** (occurring frequently and regularly)

Usage: "Every night we are disturbed by the **continual** barking of your dog," the neighbour complained.

continuous (unbroken)

Usage: He writes his name in one long, **continuous** line.

contiguous (adjacent or touching)

Usage: The **contiguous** states of the United States do not include Alaska and Hawaii.

- **cooperation** (work together for a common purpose)

Usage: Many people believe **cooperation** will help you succeed more than competition will.

corporation (a business structure)

Usage: A **corporation** is established by the authority of a state government and exists independent of the people who own it.

- **core** (central or essential part)

Usage: A good communicator emphasises the **core** of the message.

corps (a group of people who act as a body rather than as individuals)

Usage: She was satisfied to dance with the **corps** de ballet rather become a soloist.

- **costume** (specialised style of dress)

Usage: She designed a **costume** for the party.

custom (habitual practice)

Usage: In the corporate sector, business people have the **custom** of shaking hands when they meet.

- **courtesy** (politeness)

  Usage: The staff extended her every **courtesy** during her stay at the hotel.

  curtsy (bow with bended knees)

  Usage: When a woman is presented to the Queen, she is expected to **curtsy.**

- **credible** (believable)

  Usage: "Unfortunately, we don't have a **credible** witness to the crime," the cop said.

  creditable (praiseworthy)

  Usage: He did a **creditable** job in winning the contract.

  credulous (gullible)

  Usage: "What kind of **credulous** he was!" reclaimed the girl.

- **critic** (one who evaluates)

  Usage: The **critic** gave the new book a favourable review.

  critique (a formal analysis of a work)

  Usage: He sent the manuscript for **critique's** review.

- **cue** (signal to begin)

  Usage: "At the meeting, I won't say anything until I get the **cue** from you," the girl said.

  queue (people in line)

  Usage: They had to wait in the **queue** to get tickets for the movie.

- **currant** (a berry)

  Usage: The woman made some fresh **currant** jam to go with the biscuits.

current (up to date)

Usage: The **current** issue of the magazine is not yet available on the newsstands.

D

- **dairy** (having to do with milk and milk products)

  Usage: "Our best customer sells **dairy** products," the shopkeeper said.

  diary (daily record of events)

  Usage: She kept a **diary** to help her remember which baby she fed last.

- **data** (facts and figures)

  Usage: He designed a survey to collect **data** about visitors to his website.

  datum (a single fact)

  Usage: They based their measurements on the **datum** of the boiling point of water.

- **deceased** (dead)

  Usage: "I am sorry to report that our hospital records show that your uncle is **deceased**," the man said.

  diseased (seriously ill)

  Usage: The fact that he was poor and **diseased** never seemed to affect his wonderful sense of humour.

- **decent** (in good taste)

  Usage: Gestures considered **decent** in one culture may be obscene in another.

  descent (going downward)

  Usage: His **descent** from the airplane was much slower after he pulled the cord on his parachute.

  dissent (disagreement)

Usage: Of the twelve judges ruling on the case, her's was the only voice of **dissent.**

dissidence (strong disagreement and outright opposition)

Usage: The government's oppressive policies led to such **dissidence** that they were ousted in the next election.

- **decree** (official decision or order)

  Usage: The **decree** made all the striking workers return to their jobs.

  degree (step, grade or rank)

  Usage: She suffered third-**degree** burns on her arms rescuing the child.

- **decry** (to openly condemn or ridicule)

  Usage: Those who believe in a democratic society **decry** tyranny in any form.

  descry (to see or catch sight of, often from a distance)

  Usage: When the man **descried** the island, he shouted, "Land Ho!"

- **deduce** (form an opinion from a solid basis of fact)

  Usage: "From the size of these shoeprints, I **deduce** the intruder was wearing large shoes," said the detective.

  deduct (subtract)

  Usage: "Please **deduct** this amount from my bill," the man said.

- **defer** (delay or postpone; yield out of respect)

  Usage: They can **defer** the charges far one month.

  Usage: "I **defer** to my colleague's greater experience in this field," the lecturer said.

  differ (disagree)

  Usage: "I must **differ** with you about the meaning of that word," she said.

- **deference** (courteous regard)

  Usage: The young people in that family showed great **deference** for their elders.

  difference (distinguishing characteristic)

  Usage: The **difference** is that their webpages load faster than before.

- **deposition** (sworn, written statement)

  Usage: Before the start of the trial, each of the witnesses gave a **deposition** of their testimony.

  disposition (tendency to react in a certain way; final settlement)

  Usage: Pollyanna had an especially cheerful **disposition.**

  Usage: The **disposition** of her father's estate took a long time.

- **depraved** (extreme departure from what is normal and good)

  Usage: Rahul was a **depraved** student.

  deprived (take away from)

  Usage: He claimed that, during his childhood, he was **deprived** of any warmth and affection.

- **deprecate** (belittle)

  Usage: "Have you noticed that he seems to **deprecate** himself?" she asked.

  depreciate (fall in value or price)

  Usage: A new car will start to **depreciate** as soon as you drive it off the lot.

- **desert** (hot, dry, sandy place; abandon or forsake)

  Usage: Not all kinds of plants can grow in a **desert.**

  Usage: The man refused to **desert** the girl in distress.

- **dessert** (end of a meal, usually something sweet)

  Usage: They ordered ice cream for **dessert.**

- **desolate** (deserted or uninhabited; miserable)

  Usage: They washed up on the shore of a **desolate** island.

  Usage: She was in a **desolate** condition when the cops reached the place.

  dissolute (characterised by loose moral standards)

  Usage: The younger son led a **dissolute** lifestyle before he returned home to his family.

- **detract** (take something away from the value or reputation of)

  Usage: Words that are not properly used can **detract** from a writer's credibility.

  distract (divert attention from)

  Usage: A blinking graphic can **distract** attention.

- **device** (invention)

  Usage: "If your **device** works, I think you should get a patent for it," he said.

  devise (think up a way to do something new)

  Usage: He **devised** a plan to draw money from them.

- **dew** (moisture)

  Usage: It was a beautiful spring morning, and the grass sparkled with **dew.**

  do (make, cause, perform, carry out or act)

  Usage: "What shall I **do** to convince them?" she asked.

  due (payable)

  Usage: The rent is **due** the first of every month.

- **die** (stop living or existing; device for shaping)

Usage: The doctor said without an operation the patient would surely **die.**

Usage: He used to be a tool-and-**die** maker before the terrible accident.

- **dye** (colour)

  Usage: "I think I will **dye** my hair a lighter shade," the girl said.

- **disapprove** (view with disfavour)

  Usage: His parents **disapprove** of his truancy.

  disprove (prove to be false)

  Usage: The accused was determined to **disprove** the charges against him.

- **disassemble** (take apart)

  Usage: It was easy to **disassemble** the clock, but it wasn't so easy to put it back together again.

  dissemble (disguise or conceal the real nature of)

  Usage: "I'd rather be honest about my shortcomings than **dissemble** or pretend to be something I'm not," he asserted.

- **disburse** (pay out funds)

  Usage: The foundation was supposed to **disburse** the funds.

  disperse (scatter)

  Usage: The security guards told the crowd to **disperse** or face arrest.

- **discreet** (prudent, trustworthy)

  Usage: A **discreet** accountant is a valuable business asset.

  discrete (separate and distinct)

  Usage: The company is composed of three **discrete** units.

- **disinterested** (not influenced by personal motives)

Usage: "To mediate this argument, we need a **disinterested** person," the chairman said.

uninterested (unconcerned)

Usage: "I knew she was sick because she was **uninterested** in food," the woman said.

- **divers** (various, several)

  Usage: They went to visit officies of **divers** nationalities.

  diverse (markedly different or conspicuously contrasting)

  Usage: His hobbies are as **diverse** as whitewater-rafting and needlepoint.

- **done** (completed)

  Usage: She wanted the work **done** as soon as possible.

  dun (demand repeatedly)

  Usage: The collection agency went to great lengths to **dun** him for the payment.

E

- **edition** (published version)

  Usage: Read the latest **edition** of the book.

  addition (something added)

  Usage: They toured the **addition** to the hospital yesterday.

- **effect** (immediate or direct result; bring about)

  Usage: "What **effect** does that medicine have on you?" the doctor asked.

  Usage: He braided the bed sheets to **effect** an escape.

  affect (to act upon or influence)

  Usage: Strong emotions can **affect** your health.

- **effective** (producing the desired result)

  Usage: He has an **effective** introduction in his presentation.

efficient (producing the desired result with least waste)

Usage: His solutions provided **efficient** use of resources.

- **elapse** [(of time) pass by]

  Usage: Three minutes **elapsed** before her page completely loaded.

  lapse (to slip or fall; to lose effect)

  Usage: When the announcement came, all the students **lapsed** into silence.

  Usage: Your insurance policy will **lapse** if you don't pay the premiums.

  relapse (a slip backwards)

  Usage: Just when the thought he was going to get well, he suffered a **relapse**.

- **elicit** (draw out)

  Usage: The band's performances always **elicit** praise from the critics.

  illicit (not allowed)

  Usage: Illicit copying of another person's work is punishable by law.

- **eligible** (qualified for)

  Usage: "Every person who submits a new word this month is **eligible** to win the prize," they announced.

- **illegible** (hard to read)

  Usage: The professor scolded the student for his **illegible** handwriting.

  ineligible (legally disqualified)

  Usage: In the U.S., a president who has been elected twice is **ineligible** to run again.

- **elusive** (hard to catch or grasp)

Usage: The solution to the problem proved more **elusive** than they first thought.

illusive (deceptive or unreal)

Usage: Lost in the desert, he saw an **illusive** oasis called a mirage.

- **emerge** (come out of something enclosed)

  Usage: Out of four candidates, he **emerged** as their favourite.

  immerge (plunge into)

  Usage: Immerge the burn in cold water to minimise the skin damage.

  immerse (plunge into)

  Usage: Sometimes we get so **immersed** in our work, we forget how much time has elapsed.

- **emigrate** (move out of a country)

  Usage: They decided to **emigrate** to New Zealand while the children were still young.

  immigrate (move into a country)

  Usage: That lady **immigrated** to America from Lithuania.

- **emanate** (flow out from)

  Usage: She was so creative that ideas just seemed to **emanate** from her.

  eminent (outstanding)

  Usage: Steven Hawking is one of the most **eminent** thinkers of all time.

- **imminent** (impending)

  Usage: When she heard a storm was **imminent,** she backed up her work and unplugged the computer.

- **en route** (on the way)

Usage: En route to town to sell the cow, Sohan traded the cow for some magic beans.

root (underground part of a plant; origin or source; cheer for or wish success for)

Usage: Carrot is a **root** vegetable.

Usage: You can't solve a problem until you get to its **root.**

Usage: The captain **rooted** his team for the game.

rout (terrible defeat)

Usage: The Super Bowl turned out to be a complete **rout.**

route (a path which is planned and followed regularly)

Usage: "I'm thinking of supplementing my salary with a newspaper **route,**" the boy said.

- **envelop** (surround completely)

  Usage: The kids saw the python slithering forward to **envelop** its prey and crush it.

  envelope (container for a letter)

  Usage: "Please send a long, self-addressed, stamped **envelope** with your request," the woman announced.

- **equable** (even or equal and uniform)

  Usage: They are planning to create an **equable** taxation system.

  equitable (fair and just)

  Usage: The injured party sought an **equitable** settlement.

- **erasable** (capable of being rubbed out or removed)

  Usage: They ordered for some **erasable** pens.

  irascible (easily provoked to anger)

  Usage: After years of enduring chronic pain, he became so **irascible** that it took courage to visit him.

- **especially** (standing apart uniquely from the rest)

Usage: The product samples he brought were **especially** good.

specially (given unusual treatment)

Usage: The candidates were asked to look in the **specially**-marked boxes for the entry blank.

- **every day** (each day without exception)

  Usage: Every day, he goes to the shop to buy cans.

  everyday (ordinary)

  Usage: Wear your **everyday** clothes to school, and save your finest for special occasions.

- **every one** (each one, without exception)

  Usage: "Mom bought a dozen eggs yesterday and **every one** was cracked when we got home," said the kid.

  everyone (everybody)

  Usage: Everyone at the office feared the boss' reaction.

- **ewe** (female sheep)

  Usage: The **ewe** was bleating and looking for her lamb.

  yew (an evergreen tree)

  Usage: The finest violin bows are made of **yew** wood.

  you (the one or ones being spoken to)

  Usage: The shopkeeper said, "I guarantee that **you** will be satisfied with the product."

- **exalt** (glorify or put much higher)

  Usage: In ancient Egypt, the Pharaoh was **exalted** over his subjects.

  exult (rejoice)

  Usage: The winning team went to the restaurant to **exult** in their victory.

- **exceed** (to go past a stated limit)

Usage: It is illegal to **exceed** the speed limit.

accede (give in to; take a position of authority)

Usage: We **accede** to your demands.

Usage: "When did the King **accede** to the throne?" he asked.

- **expand** (enlarge)

  Usage: One reason for a business to have a website is to **expand** its market.

  expend (pay out money)

  Usage: They didn't consider it necessary to **expend** any money or time on marketing.

- **expansive** (broad)

  Usage: Their **expansive** front lawn was the envy of the neighbourhood.

  expensive (costing a lot of money)

  Usage: The arrangements for the wedding were rather **expensive.**

- **expatiate** (write or speak in great detail)

  Usage: Before beginning, he said, "Please forgive me if I **expatiate,** but this is what I want to talk about."

  expiate (atone for or make amends for)

  Usage: She devoted her life to charity to try to **expiate** the wrongs of her youth.

- **extant** (still existing)

  Usage: The museum has the last **extant** copy of the manuscript.

  extent (the limit to which something extends)

  Usage: The **extent** of the universe seems to grow as our ability to make better telescopes grows.

F

- **facet** (any of several sides or aspects of something)

  Usage: Professionals carefully considered every **facet** of the problem.

  faucet (spigot or tap)

  Usage: The dripping of the **faucet** kept the man awake.

- **facetious** (something funny or not serious)

  Usage: His father didn't like his **facetious** remarks about such a serious subject.

  factitious (artificial)

  Usage: Her **factitious** laughter didn't fool anyone.

  fictitious (imaginary)

  Usage: This story is completely **fictitious.**

- **facilitate** (make easy)

  Usage: Computers have **facilitated** a lot of daily operations.

  felicitate (congratulate)

  Usage: His parents called long-distance to **felicitate** the happy couple.

- **facility** (ease of doing something; something made to serve a function)

  Usage: The gymnast showed her **facility** with the parallel bars.

  Usage: "Visitors are invited to tour our new kitchen **facility,**" said the hotel manager.

  felicity (great happiness)

  Usage: The trip to the country was a time of **felicity** for the kid.

- **faint** (lose consciousness)

Usage: "For a minute, I thought I was going to **faint**," said the model.

feint (pretend to strike a blow)

Usage: His strategy was to **feint** with his right hand while preparing to deliver a mighty blow with his left.

- **fair** (exhibition or marketplace)

  Usage: They bought these baskets at the local farmers' **fair.**

  fare (cost of a ride in a vehicle)

  Usage: They wanted to know the **fare** for going by plane.

  fare (experience good or bad results)

  Usage: "We'll see how our business **fares** with the new marketing plan," they said.

- **farther** (more distant)

  Usage: "Each day I try to walk a little **farther** than the day before," he said.

  further (additional or more)

  Usage: If there are no **further** questions, they will adjourn the meeting.

- **faze** (scare or worry)

  Usage: The warnings on the television didn't seem to **faze** him at all.

  phase (aspect or stage of development)

  Usage: Most two-year-olds go through a rebellious **phase.**

- **feat** (a noteworthy deed)

  Usage: Her performance on the ice concluded with a remarkable **feat** of agility and speed.

  feet (plural of foot)

  Usage: The child kept swinging his **feet.**

- **finale** (concluding part)

Usage: They missed the **finale,** as they were late.

finally (in the end)

Usage: After competing many times, he **finally** won the gold medal.

finely (excellently; in small pieces)

Usage: She stood out from the others because she was **finely** dressed.

Usage: "For extra flavour add one cup **finely** chopped onions," said the chef.

- **fineness** (state or quality of being nearly perfect)

  Usage: The gold jewelry he brought was of exquisite **fineness.**

  finesse (tactfulness or smoothness)

  Usage: Salespersons must handle customers with utmost **finesse.**

- **fir** (type of evergreen tree)

  Usage: He planted a **fir** tree in the front yard.

  fur (animal hair)

  Usage: He liked the cat because of its **fur.**

- **fiscal** (financial)

  Usage: The **fiscal** year begins April 1.

  physical (relating to the body or the material world)

  Usage: He is preparing for the **physical** examination.

- **flair** (talent)

  Usage: You have a **flair** for the dramatic.

  flare (a signalling device using bright light; outward spread)

  Usage: They used a **flare** gun to tell the rescue team where to find us.

  Usage: The **flare** of her nostrils signalled her anger.

- **flaunt** (make a showy display)

  Usage: It is considered rude to **flaunt** one's wealth in front of others.

  flout (treat with contempt)

  Usage: Rebellious youths **flout** authority.

- **flounder** (struggle clumsily)

  Usage: She **floundered** around the room, looking for an old book.

  founder (sink, collapse or fail completely)

  Usage: The iceberg caused the ocean liner Titanic to **founder.**

- **flour** (ground wheat powder)

  Usage: Make a paste of **flour** and water.

  flower (a blossom)

  Usage: The child handed his mother a **flower.**

- **flew** (past tense of fly)

  Usage: The birds **flew** south every winter.

  flu (short–term for influenza)

  Usage: He didn't go to work because he had **flu.**

  flue (passage to let air or gas escape)

  Usage: "Don't block the chimney **flue** or the house will fill with smoke," instructed the woman.

- **for** (a preposition meaning on account of or because of)

  Usage: She was fired **for** stealing.

  fore (at or to the front)

  Usage: Out of all the software makers in the world, his company has come to the **fore.**

  four (one more than three)

  Usage: They have **four** children in the family.

- **forbear** (abstain or refrain from)

  Usage: "I will **forbear** mentioning his name again," she said.

  forebear (ancestor)

  Usage: Most people have at least one **forebear** they admire.

- **foregoing** (preceding)

  Usage: The **foregoing** paragraph is about the words forbear and forebear.

  forgoing (doing without)

  Usage: "To save time, we are **forgoing** the usual formalities," they said.

- **foreword** (introduction in a book, which is usually brief and simple)

  Usage: A noted scholar wrote the **foreword.**

  forward (onward or toward the front)

  Usage: Despite the obstacles, he kept moving **forward** to his goal.

- **formally** (done in a valid and binding way)

  Usage: They **formally** announced their engagement a month ago.

  formerly (previously)

  Usage: She was **formerly** the mayor of D.M.C.

- **fort** (military post)

  Usage: The **fort** was surrounded.

  forte (something in which a person excels)

  Usage: His **forte** is design and hers is business, so they make a great team.

- **forth** (forward)

  Usage: She came **forth** to meet him.

fourth (next after third)

Usage: That was the **fourth** time they had met.

G

- **genius** (person with exceptional intelligence or talent)

  Usage: That painting was made by a **genius**.

  genus (kind, sort or classification)

  Usage: The dog, the wolf, and the coyote belong to the same **genus.**

- **grate** (a framework of iron bars; scrape or shred)

  Usage: Clean out the ashes under the **grate** in the fireplace.

  Usage: She proceeded to **grate** the cheese for the dish.

  great (extraordinary or outstanding)

  Usage: You did a **great** job on your term paper.

H

- **hail** (salute, greet or call; ice shower)

  Usage: The man asked his servant to **hail** a cab.

  Usage: "We didn't get snow, but we got **hail,**" said the kid.

  hale (healthy and strong)

  Usage: Astronauts must be **hale** and hearty people to cope with the hardships of space travel.

- **hall** (passageway or a large room)

  Usage: The arrangement in the **hall** were appreciated by all.

  haul (drag or transport)

  Usage: He earned extra money by using his truck to **haul** vegetables to the local farmers' fair.

- **heal** (mend or restore to health)

Usage: "Keep the wound clean and dry and it will **heal** in a few days," said the doctor.

heel (part of a foot or part of a shoe)

Usage: She couldn't walk, as she had a blister on her **heel.**

- **hear** (perceive by ear)

  Usage: They will **hear** the noise at the set time.

  here (in this place)

  Usage: She came **here** to study.

- **heard** (past tense of hear)

  Usage: We **heard** the news and were shocked.

  herd (flock or large group of animals)

  Usage: The younger elephants stayed in the centre of the **herd** for protection.

- **holly** (plant of the Ilex genus)

  Usage: They have a hedge of **holly** bushes on their property.

  holy (sacred or pure)

  Usage: The people refused to build there because they considered it **holy** ground.

  wholly (completely or entirely)

  Usage: The work was **wholly** done by the little boy.

- **human** (of mankind)

  Usage: Imagination is a **human** trait.

  humane (kind and good)

  Usage: They joined a group of students working for more **humane** treatment of animals.

I

- **ideal** (mental image of perfection or excellence)

  Usage: They set a high **ideal** for the job.

idle (inactive or ineffective)

Usage: "She works all the time; I've never seen her **idle,**" he said.

idol (object that people worship)

Usage: He donated the golden **idol** he found to the museum.

idyll (pastoral poem or story)

Usage: The peaceful countryside looked like it would be a perfect setting for an **idyll.**

- **in to** (two words, an adverb and a preposition)

  Usage: Even though it was supposed to be her day off, she came **in to** finish her monthly report.

  into (entering or changing form)

  Usage: She drove **into** the parking lot and found a space.

- **incidence** (frequency of occurrence)

  Usage: The plant was disapproved, as there was a high **incidence** of cancer near it.

  incidents (events or happenings)

  Usage: Some sad **incidents** kept him back.

- **incite** (motivate)

  Usage: We should **incite** one another to love fine works.

  insight (understanding)

  Usage: His **insight** into the problems and suggestions gained him respect and admiration.

- **ingenious** (clever, imaginative or inventive)

  Usage: The teacher gave an **ingenious** solution to the math problem.

  ingenuous (candid, frank or guileless)

Usage: They grew to love him because of his sincere and **ingenuous** nature.

- **inhabit** (live in or on)

  Usage: Many rare animals **inhabit** the island.

  inhibit (hold back or restrain)

  Usage: Cleanliness will **inhibit** the growth of germs.

- **instance** (case or example)

  Usage: The group supported him in that **instance.**

  instants (very short periods of time)

  Usage: "I looked away for just a few **instants,** and when I looked back he was gone," she said.

- **intelligent** (able to understand and to reason well)

  Usage: Her answer showed her to be an **intelligent** young woman.

  intelligible (capable of being understood)

  Usage: "With my mouth full of food, I was unable to make an **intelligible** reply to the question," the man said.

- **intense** (very strong or of a high degree)

  Usage: He had an **intense** craving for chocolate.

  intents (aims or purposes)

  Usage: Although we see other people's actions, we don't always know their **intents.**

- **interstate** (between or among two or more states)

  Usage: Federal laws cover **interstate** commerce.

  intestate (without making a will)

  Usage: If a rich person dies **intestate,** courts decide who inherits the money.

  intrastate (within one state)

  Usage: State laws cover **intrastate** commerce.

- **it's** (contraction of it is)

  Usage: It's so nice to see you again.

  its (belonging to it)

  Usage: The cat licked **its** paw.

J

- **jibe** (agree with)

  Usage: His alibi doesn't **jibe** with the testimony of eye-witnesses.

  gibe (jeer or taunt derisively)

  Usage: "I would never **gibe** someone because it's unkind," she said.

K

- **knew** (past tense of know)

  Usage: He **knew** the results before they were declared.

  new (fresh original)

  Usage: The **new** scheme was designed to attract customers.

- **know** (recognise or be familiar with or understand)

  Usage: He wanted **know** about the man in the car.

  no (not any)

  Usage: A business with **no** customers doesn't stay in business for very long.

L

- **later** (comparative form of late)

  Usage: The boy was **later** than the rest of the students.

  latter (second of two mentioned)

  Usage: The **latter** affair in the list was mentioned first unknowingly.

- **lead** (silvery gray metal often used in pencils)

  Usage: He needed a new **lead** for his mechanical pencil.

  led (was out in front or conducted or guided)

  Usage: Their team **led** the league for two seasons.

- **leased** (contracted to use for a specified period of time)

  Usage: They decided a **leased** car was better.

  least (smallest)

  Usage: He wanted to employ them with the **least** pay package.

- **lessen** (decrease, diminish)

  Usage: Buckling your seat belt will **lessen** the chance of injury in an accident.

  lesson (unit of instruction)

  Usage: The teacher taught the boy's favourite **lesson** in the book.

- **levee** (embankment along a river to prevent flooding)

  Usage: The townspeople felt much safer once the **levee** was completed.

- **levy** (impose or collect)

  Usage: The ruler misused his right to **levy** taxes.

- **liable** (legally responsible)

  Usage: When he lost his case, he was found **liable** for crores of Rupees in damages.

  libel (maliciously damaging someone's reputation in print)

  Usage: The new author was sued for **libel** by the publisher.

- **lightening** (making brighter or less heavy or easier)

  Usage: The workers who came were meant for **lightening** the work load.

  lighting (illumination)

Usage: The room needed good **lighting** system.

lightning (flash of light that accompanies an electric discharge in the atmosphere)

Usage: Flashes of **lightning** in the night sky frightened the kid.

- **loan** (something given temporarily)

  Usage: He didn't want to take **loan** from the bank.

  lone (solitary or unaccompanied)

  Usage: The **lone** man seemed mysterious.

- **local** (limited to a particular place)

  Usage: The **local** people were amazed at the number of visitors to their town.

  locale (location, site or spot)

  Usage: The town beside the river made a charming **locale** for the author's.

- **loose** (not tight or confined)

  Usage: He let the kids **loose** and they made a mess of the room.

  lose (misplace or fail)

  Usage: One shouldn't care whether they win or **lose**. They should just enjoy playing the game.

  loss (that which is lost)

  Usage: "Even if we didn't make a very large profit this year, it's still better than a **loss**," the manager said.

M

- **made** (produced or constructed)

  Usage: They **made** a cake for the party.

  maid (female server)

  Usage: The **maid** served the tea in the parlour.

- **magnificent** (splendid or grand)

  Usage: The prince grew up in a **magnificent** palace, but he was lonely.

  munificent (extremely generous)

  Usage: He gave a Ten Lakhs rupees to the school, a **munificent** donation.

- **mail** (letters sent through the post office)

  Usage: The peon left the **mail** on the table.

  male (masculine)

  Usage: The **male** members of the house were called to help.

- **main** (principal or chief)

  Usage: His account is at the **main** office of the bank.

  mane (long hair)

  Usage: The child was asked to name two animals that have **mane**.

- **manner** (way of acting or behaving)

  Usage: "Please fill out the entry form in the prescribed **manner**," he instructed.

  manor (mansion or main house on an estate)

  Usage: He returned to the ancestral **manor** every spring.

- **marital** (relating to marriage)

  Usage: Marital happiness takes work on the part of both husband and wife.

  marshal (peace officer)

  Usage: To make sure the law was obeyed, a U.S. **marshal** stood at each entrance.

  martial (military or warlike)

Usage: During the emergency, the town came under **martial** law.

- **material** (fabric)

  Usage: The coat was made of dark blue woollen **material.**

  materiel (equipment and supplies of an army or an organisation)

  Usage: "We have one department in our company for personnel, another for **materiel,**" the secretary informed.

- **may be** [two words (verbs)]

  Usage: She said, "I **may be** wrong, but I think the store is closed."

  maybe [perhaps (adverb)]

  Usage: "**Maybe** they wanted to get a toy," he argued.

- **meat** (edible flesh of an animal)

  Usage: Vegetarians do not eat **meat.**

  meet (come together)

  Usage: The team wanted to **meet** the hotel president.

- **missed** (felt regret at someone's absence)

  Usage: I **missed** seeing you at the reunion.

  mist (fine spray)

  Usage: It wasn't a shower; it was more like a **mist.**

- **might** (physical power)

  Usage: He hit the ball with all his **might.**

  mite (a tiny insect)

  Usage: Many allergies are caused by the common dust **mite.**

- **moral** (good conduct according to a standard of right and wrong)

  Usage: The **moral** thing to do isn't always the popular thing to do.

morale (spirit or attitude)

Usage: The coach gave a pep talk to lift the team's **morale.**

- **morality** (goodness according to a recognised code of conduct)

  Usage: For their leader they chose a person of the highest **morality.**

  mortality (condition of being subject to death)

  Usage: People feared the disease because of its high **mortality** rate.

- **morning** (early part of the day)

  Usage: She eats fruits every **morning**.

- **mourning** (sorrow or grief)

  Usage: The nation entered a time of **mourning** after Prime Minister Indira Gandhi's assassination.

N

- **no body** (no group)

  Usage: No body of law enacted by humans can be called perfect.

  nobody (no person)

  Usage: Nobody raised a voice against the tyrant.

O

- **one** (single person or thing)

  Usage: The store is located on a **one**-way street.

  won (past tense of win)

  Usage: The player who **won** the gold medal gave a splendid speech.

- **ordinance** (regulation or law)

Usage: The city council passed an **ordinance** against disturbing the peace.

ordnance (military weapons and equipment)

Usage: The **ordnance** was stored in bunkers near the airfield.

- **overdo** (do too much or go too far)

  Usage: The doctor warned him not to **overdo** the exercise.

  overdue (past the expected time)

  Usage: The library books are **overdue.**

P

- **packed** (crowded together)

  Usage: The room was **packed** with party lovers.

  pact (agreement)

  Usage: The two countries signed a mutual non-aggression **pact**.

- **pail** (bucket with a handle)

  Usage: The child filled his **pail** with sand at the seashore.

  pale (lacking colour)

  Usage: She turned **pale** after abortion.

- **pain** (suffering)

  Usage: He took leave, as he had **pain** in his back.

  pane (sheet of glass set in a window)

  Usage: They had to buy a new **pane** of glass for the front window, as the kids broke it.

- **pair** (two of a kind)

  Usage: "I need a new **pair** of shoes," the boy shouted.

  pare (trim the outer layer of)

  Usage: "Do you **pare** an apple when you eat it or do you like it unpeeled?" the teacher asked.

pear (bell-shaped fruit)

Usage: She had a juicy **pear** for her lunch.

- **partition** (a divider)

  Usage: They used bookshelves as a **partition** in the large living room.

  petition (a formal request)

  Usage: She signed the **petition** to change the zoning law.

- **partially** (to some extent)

  Usage: The moon was **partially** visible due to eclipse.

  partly (in some parts)

  Usage: The car was **partly** painted.

- **patience** (ability to wait without complaining)

  Usage: Teaching children requires a lot of **patience**.

  patients (people undergoing medical care)

  Usage: The doctor visits **patients** in the hospital.

- **peace** (absence of war or troubles)

  Usage: She works hard to make her home a place of rest and **peace** for her family.

  piece (separate part of a whole)

  Usage: He wanted the last **piece** of the pie.

- **peal** (loud, prolonged sound)

  Usage: The **peal** of the bells woke everyone.

  peel (outer covering of a fruit or vegetable)

  Usage: He wanted the kid to **peel** the banana.

- **peer** (an equal)

  Usage: When it comes to playing the tabla, he has no **peer**.

  pier (landing place for ships)

Usage: They waved from the **pier** as the cruise ship sailed.

- **perfect** (free from defects or complete)

  Usage: The sweater is a **perfect** fit.

  prefect (high-ranking official)

  Usage: He made an appointment to interview the **prefect** about the new policy.

- **persecute** (oppress or harass)

  Usage: The slave was **persecuted** regularly.

  prosecute (conduct legal proceedings against)

  Usage: The minister was **prosecuted** for all the wrong reasons.

- **personal** (private)

  Usage: She didn't want to discuss her **personal** affairs in a public place.

  personnel (Human Resources department of a company)

  Usage: The resumes were forwarded to the **personnel** department.

- **perspective** (point of view)

  Usage: From his **perspective**, it looks unfair.

  prospective (expected or future)

  Usage: The **prospective** buyer went to the company's website to learn about the new product.

- **peruse** (read all the way through carefully)

  Usage: The head of the department set aside time to **peruse** the report before making a decision.

  pursue (chase or follow for a specific purpose)

  Usage: You must be willing to **pursue** your goal despite setbacks if you want to succeed.

- **plain** (clear and distinct; flat, level ground)

  Usage: The facts he presented were **plain**.

  Usage: The ground they selected for the purpose was **plain**.

  plane (aircraft)

  Usage: They wanted to go by **plane**.

- **pleas** (earnest requests or appeals)

  Usage: His **pleas** for help brought the rescuers quickly.

  please (be agreeable to)

  Usage: The boy wanted to **please** the girl with flowers and chocolates.

- **pole** (long, slender, wooden rod)

  Usage: He got his fishing **pole** and went down to the lake.

  poll (survey of public opinion)

  Usage: The **poll** showed that their candidate took the lead.

- **populace** (all the inhabitants of a place)

  Usage: The circus entertained the **populace** with a huge parade through town.

  populous (having many inhabitants)

  Usage: The new reforms had rules for **populous** areas.

- **portend** (indicate beforehand)

  Usage: The gray clouds did not **portend** a sunny afternoon for the picnic.

  pretend (give a false show of)

  Usage: Most children like to dress up and **pretend** they are adults.

- **pray** (entreat or call upon a higher power)

  Usage: Many people **pray** before eating a meal.

  prey (victimise)

Usage: Confidence men and women **prey** on unwary, trusting people.

- **precede** (to go or come before)

  Usage: The bridesmaids **precede** the bride down the aisle at a wedding.

  proceed (move ahead)

  Usage: The group would **proceed** to the ground after lunch.

- **precedence** (act of coming before)

  Usage: The need for safety took **precedence** over everything else.

  precedents (actions that serve as patterns for future actions)

  Usage: The judge could find no **precedents** that would allow him to find the defendant innocent.

- **presence** (state of being at a specific place)

  Usage: "Your **presence** is requested at the wedding of our daughter," the man said.

  presents (gifts)

  Usage: To show how happy she was, she bought **presents** for all her friends.

- **principal** (head of a school; amount of money borrowed)

  Usage: The **principal** of the school scolded the boys.

  Usage: Interest will be charged on the **principal** at the rate of 6.9 per cent.

  principle (fundamental law or basic truth)

  Usage: The teacher fumbled while explaining the **principle** of earth's gravity.

- **profit** (amount left after all costs of a business are paid)

  Usage: The company made great **profits** in that year.

prophet (one who foretells the future or interprets divine will)

Usage: A **prophet** was welcomed in their house.

Q

- **quiet** (not noisy)

  Usage: It was a **quiet** and cozy room.

  quit (discontinue or resign)

  Usage: She decided to **quit** the play after the argument.

  quite (completely or to a considerable degree)

  Usage: The man was **quite** right about the people over board.

R

- **rain** (water falling as drops from the sky)

  Usage: The match was postponed due to **rain.**

  reign (rule as a monarch)

  Usage: The country prospered under his **reign.**

- **raise** (lift or elevate)

  Usage: She was so eager to give the answer that she forgot to **raise** her hand.

  rays (narrow beams of light)

  Usage: The **rays** of sunlight through the blinds woke her up early in the morning.

  raze (demolish)

  Usage: The party went to **raze** the factory.

- **rap** (knock or tap sharply)

  Usage: He was asked to **rap** on the door again.

  wrap (to put a cover around something)

Usage: The woman rushed to **wrap** the child in a blanket.

- **read** (understand something written)

  Usage: When all else fails, **read** the instruction manual.

  read (past tense of to read)

  Usage: He **read** the letter again to make sure he hadn't misunderstood.

  reed (tall grass found in marshes or part of a musical instrument)

  Usage: He needed to buy a new **reed** for his clarinet.

  red (a colour)

  Usage: She wore a **red** dress for the party.

- **real** (actual, true or genuine)

  Usage: The ladies wondered whether her necklace was made of **real** pearls.

  reel (wind up a line)

  Usage: When the fish gets tired you can **reel** it in.

- **reality** (fact)

  Usage: The **reality** brought dire images in his mind.

  realty (land and buildings on it)

  Usage: They went to the **realty** office to look at listings for new homes.

- **recent** (just before now or of a time not long past)

  Usage: His article was in the **recent** issue of the magazine.

  resent (feel bitterness toward)

  Usage: They **resent** being called fools.

- **residence** (place where one lives)

  Usage: The suspect left his **residence** around noon.

  residents (inhabitants)

Usage: The **residents** of the little town were sad to see the visitors leave.

- **retch** (to try to vomit)

  Usage: The awful smell made the girl **retch.**

  wretch (a pitiful or despised person)

  Usage: The people beat the **wretch** who snatched the chain.

- **right** (correct or accurate)

  Usage: Careful writers strive to use the **right** word.

  rite (customary and solemn ritual or ceremony)

  Usage: The **rite** of baptism is taken very seriously in many faiths.

  write (to mark letters or symbols on a surface with a tool)

  Usage: The students were asked to **write** down the notes in their books.

- **role** (position or function)

  Usage: The manager asked about his **role** in the new company.

- **roll** (move by wheels; piece of bread; list of names)

  Usage: "**Roll** this car forward," he shouted.

  Usage: "I'd like a buttered **roll** with my soup," she said.

  Usage: The teacher forgot to take **roll** today.

- **rote** (unthinking routine)

  Usage: Foreign languages used to be taught by the **rote** method.

  wrote (past tense of write)

  Usage: The man **wrote** to the company last week.

S

- **sail** (canvas sheet attached to a boat)

Usage: The **sail** of the boat was torn beyond repair.

sale (transfer of ownership for a price)

Usage: Everything on the counter was for **sale**.

- **scene** (place where something happened)

  Usage: The detectives roped off the **scene** of the crime.

  seen (past participle of to see)

  Usage: The party members were angry, as they had **seen** their leader drunk.

- **seam** (line formed by joining two edges)

  Usage: Every **seam** bulged when he tried on his old army uniform.

  seem (appear to be)

  Usage: The children **seem** to be healthy.

- **serge** (a kind of fabric)

  Usage: He wore a navy blue **serge** suit for the meeting.

  surge (a strong forward movement)

  Usage: When the doors opened there was a **surge** in the crowd.

- **so** (in such a manner or very much)

  Usage: He was **so** tired that he lay down the moment he entered the house.

  sow (scatter seeds)

  Usage: Farmers will reap the same type of crop that they **sow.**

- **shear** (cut off)

  Usage: "It is time for us to **shear** the wool from the sheep," said the man.

  sheer (transparent; pure, unmixed with anything else)

Usage: Women usually wear **sheer** hosiery in warm weather.

Usage: That was an act of **sheer** stupidity!

- **shone** (past tense of shine)

  Usage: Yesterday, the sun **shone** brightly.

  shown (past participle of show)

  Usage: Smoking has been **shown** to be bad for health.

- **sleight** (skill and dexterity)

  Usage: Magicians fool people with **sleight** of hand.

  slight (slender)

  Usage: The weather forecaster predicted a **slight** chance of rain.

- **soar** (fly upward)

  Usage: The kids watched the eagle **soar** into the sky and disappear.

  sore (painful)

  Usage: He didn't go for a walk, as he had **sore** feet.

- **soared** (flew upward or rose very high)

  Usage: Their spirits **soared** when they heard about the award they received.

  sword (a long, pointed weapon)

  Usage: The knight buckled on his **sword** and went to the battle.

- **sole** (bottom part of the foot or shoe; only one)

  Usage: They laughed on seeing a hole in the **sole** of her shoe.

  Usage: She is the **sole** proprietor of her business.

  soul (person)

  Usage: Not a **soul** was in the room when the man arrived.

- **son** (male child)

  Usage: He took his **son** and daughter to the office to teach them about industry.

  sun (star that provides heat and light to the earth)

  Usage: Too much exposure to the **sun** can damage skin.

- **spacious** (roomy)

  Usage: She invited her friends into her **spacious** living room.

  specious (counterfeit)

  Usage: Be careful, as he is known for using **specious** arguments to back up his claims.

- **staid** (conservative or sedate)

  Usage: She was hardened by their **staid** beliefs.

  stayed (past tense of stay)

  Usage: Her parents **stayed** by her side through all the trouble.

- **stair** (a step)

  Usage: The carpet was loose on the first **stair**.

  stare (gaze fixedly)

  Usage: The girl reprimanded the man and asked him not to **stare.**

- **stake** (strong stick or post)

  Usage: A young tree may be tied to a **stake** for support.

  steak (a slice of meat or fish)

  Usage: When they went out for dinner, he ordered **steak.**

- **stationary** (in the same place)

  Usage: It was fine till the car was **stationary**.

  stationery (writing paper and envelopes)

Usage: He opened a **stationery** shop to support his family.

- **steal** (commit a theft)

  Usage: The burglars came to **steal** the diamond.

  steel (alloy of iron noted for strength)

  Usage: The **steel** utensils they brought were meant for the newly wed couple.

T

- **tacked** (use a small nail with broad, flat head to attach)

  Usage: The principal **tacked** the message to inform the students about the new rules.

  tact (diplomacy)

  Usage: This difficult situation must be handled with **tact** and sensitivity.

- **tail** (last part)

  Usage: The veterinarian examined the dog from head to **tail.**

  tale (story)

  Usage: The children coaxed their grandmother into narrating them the **tale** of Lord Rama.

- **tear** (rip)

  Usage: The letter made her so angry that she wanted to **tear** it into pieces.

  tear (drop of fluid from the eye)

  Usage: **Tears** rolled down her eyes as she saw him coming.

  tier (layer or row of a vertical arrangement)

  Usage: The kids were happy to sit in the top **tier** of seats in the stadium.

- **taught** (past tense of teach)

Usage: The experience **taught** him to obey rules.

taut (stretched tight)

Usage: The rope was pulled **taut** between the two poles.

- **team** (a group working together in a united action)

  Usage: The **team** project got completed before time.

  teem (be full)

  Usage: The lakes in that region **teem** with all kinds of fish.

- **tenant** (one who holds the right to occupy a place)

  Usage: Mr. Sharma talked about his new **tenant.**

  tenet (a rule or part of a body of doctrine)

  Usage: The sanctity of marriage is an important **tenet** of her faith.

- **than** (a conjunction in sentences involving comparison)

  Usage: The girls performed better **than** the boys.

  then (at that time or in that case)

  Usage: "If you agree that my skills and experience are what you need to do this job, **then** let's draw up the contract," said the man.

- **their** (belonging to them)

  Usage: The man and the woman prayed, as **their** son was in the hospital.

  there (in that place)

  Usage: "Set the box **there** on the counter," ordered the lady.

  they're (contraction of they are)

  Usage: She said **they're** coming for dinner next Monday night.

- **theirs** (belong to them, used when no noun follows)

  Usage: There can be no doubt the money is **theirs.**

  there's (contraction of there is)

  Usage: The evidence is clear, so **there's** no use denying it.

- **thorough** (not leaving anything out)

  Usage: The police conducted a **thorough** search of the apartment, looking for clues.

  threw (past tense of throw)

  Usage: The news **threw** the whole office into a panic.

  through (from the beginning to the end)

  Usage: The manager walked **through** the store during lunch hour.

- **to** (toward)

  Usage: He met with an accident while going **to** the site.

  too (in addition or very much)

  Usage: He was **too** harsh with the students.

  two (the number after one)

  Usage: The **two** candidates for the job were sent back.

- **tortuous** (twisting)

  Usage: The cabin was reached by a **tortuous** mountain road.

  torturous (full of torture)

  Usage: The man grumbled, as he had a **torturous** toothache.

- **trail** (path or remnants of passage)

  Usage: The woman's journey through life left a **trail** of broken promises.

trial (time of testing or judging)

Usage: He was kept hushed by his lawyer throughout the **trial.**

U

- **undo** (cancel or reverse what has been done)

  Usage: We have the **undo** option to rectify mistakes done on the computer.

  undue (beyond what is appropriate)

  Usage: The teacher laid **undue** stress on the students.
- **urban** (relating to a city or city life)

  Usage: She was a specialist in **urban** planning.

  urbane (refined and sophisticated)

  Usage: Years in the foreign diplomatic service gave him **urbane** manners.

V

- **vain** (ineffective)

  Usage: Their efforts to keep their position seemed **vain** when the new ruling came.

  vein (blood vessel; mood or tendency)

  Usage: The surgeon looked for the **vein** to draw blood.

  Usage: She likes reading stories that have a humorous **vein.**
- **vale** (valley)

  Usage: The flowers in the **vale** looked beautiful.

  veil (covering or curtain)

  Usage: She wore a heavy veil to conceal her puffy, red eyes.
- **veracity** (truthfulness)

Usage: The **veracity** of the matter was proved only after the woman came with sufficient proofs.

voracity (eagerness or great hunger)

Usage: She loves mystery books so much that she reads them with **voracity.**

W

- **wail** (to cry loudly, expressing sorrow)

  Usage: The man couldn't stand seeing the baby **wail** through the night.

  whale (any of the larger cetacean mammals)

  Usage: Moby Dick is an adventurous story about a man looking desperately for a **whale.**

- **waist** (the part of a human body between the ribs and the hips)

  Usage: Her **waist** was just too thin.

  waste (act of squandering)

  Usage: They took sufficient measures to avoid any sort of **waste.**

- **wait** (period of expectation or the act of waiting)

  Usage: They had to **wait** for the chief guest to arrive.

  weight (heaviness)

  Usage: "It feels good to sit down and take the **weight** off my feet," said the man.

- **waiver** (voluntary relinquishment of a right)

  Usage: The university gave him a **waiver** for the payment of tuition.

  waver (go back and forth on a decision)

  Usage: "We must decide today—there's no more time to **waver,**" she pleaded.

- **want** (have a desire for)

  Usage: Old people **want** to be loved and cared for.

  wont (customary practice or habit)

  Usage: It was his **wont** to stay late at the office.

  won't (contraction meaning will not)

  Usage: The boss called, saying he **won't** be in until ten.

- **way** (course of action or manner)

  Usage: They wanted to know the **way** to the new hotel.

  weigh (measure the heaviness of)

  Usage: It's a good idea to use the same scale each time you **weigh** yourself.

- **weak** (having little strength)

  Usage: The girl felt **weak** because she hadn't eaten all day.

  week (period of seven days)

  Usage: The **week** ended with a grand party.

- **weather** (climate)

  Usage: The **weather** was beautiful when they came out.

  whether (conjunction before the first of two choices)

  Usage: "I can't decide **whether** I want to sell the property or keep it," he expressed.

- **who ever** (who is used as a pronoun and ever is used as an adverb)

  Usage: "**Who ever** goes to that haunted place!" the girl reclaimed.

  whoever (anyone who)

  Usage: "**Whoever** wants this contract can have it," he said.

- **who's** (contraction of who is or who has)

  Usage: "**Who's** been reading my notebook?" the boy called out.

  whose (belonging to who)

  Usage: He wanted to know **whose** book was on the table.

Y

- **you're** (contraction meaning you are)

  Usage: He said to the girl, "**You're** a true gem!"

  your (belonging to you)

  Usage: "I thank you for **your** compliments," replied the girl.

CHAPTER 7

Some Technical Words

Certain subjects like Science, Maths, Geography, etc. use some technical terms. Have a look at how to remember their spellings without any mistake.

Spelling Science Related Words

Here are some words that you'll come across in Science. Use this chart as a guide to memorise all of them.

Word	Syllables	Difficult Parts
Absorb	ab-sorb	
Acid	ac-id	acid
Alkaline	al-ka-line	alkaline (unclear vowel sound)
Amphibian	am-phi-bi-an	**-ph- -bi-**
Apparatus	ap-par-a-tus	double p
Chemical	chem-i-cal	**ch-**
Circulate	cir-cu-late	starts like circle
Circulation	cir-cu-la-tion	
Combustion	com-bus-tion	don't forget the -t-
Condensation	con-dens-a-tion	
Digest	di-gest	**-g-** for the j sound
Digestion	di-ges-tion	
Disperse	dis-perse	**-er-**

Dissolve	dis-solve	double **-ss-**
Distil	dis-til	only one **-l-**
Distillation	dis-til-la-tion	double **-ll-**
Element	el-e-ment	the second **-e-** sounds bit like **-a-**
Evaporation	e-vap-or-a-tion	
Frequency	fre-quen-cy	fre- (only one e)
Friction	fric-tion	
Function	func-tion	**-c-** not -k-
Hazard	ha-zard	**-z-**
Laboratory	la-bor-a-tor-y	second **-a-** unclear vowel sound
Nutrient	nu-tri-ent	
Organism	or-gan-is-m	
Oxygen	ox-y-gen	**-y-** and **-g-**
Particle	par-tic-le	
Predator	pre-da-tor	**-or** (not -er)
Respiration	res-pir-a-tion	**-pir-**
Solution	sol-u-tion	**sol-** unclear vowel sound
Temperature	tem-per-a-ture	pronounce it clearly
Thermometer	ther-mo-me-ter	
Vertebrate	ver-teb-rate	-teb- unclear vowel sound

Spelling Maths Related Words

Here are some words that you'll come across in Maths. Use this chart as a guide to memorise all of them.

Word	Syllables	Difficult Parts
Addition	add-i-tion	remember **-dd-**
Approximately	ap-prox-i-mate-ly	**-pp-**

Average	a-ver-age	**-age** unclear vowel sound
Calculate	cal-cu-late	
Centimetre	cent-i-me-tre	
Circumference	cir-cum-fer-ence	begins like circle
Co-ordinate	co-ord-i-nate	remember hyphen: **o-o**
Diameter	di-a-me-ter	ending: **-ter** (not tre)
Digit	dig-it	**-g-** for the j sound
Equilateral	e-qui-lat-er-al	don't leave out second -e
Estimate	es-tim-ate	
Fraction	frac-tion	
Guess	guess	don't forget silent **-u-**
Horizontal	ho-riz-on-tal	**-tal** (not tle)
Isosceles	i-sos-ce-les	**-sc- -les**
Measure	mea-sure	**mea-** tricky vowel sound
Multiplication	mul-ti-pli-ca-tion	
Parallel	par-al-lel	**-ll-**
Parallelogram	par-al-lel-o-gram	(easy when you break it up into syllables)
Negative	neg-a-tive	
Perimeter	per-i-me-ter	ending: **-ter** (not tre)
Perpendicular	per-pen-dic-u-lar	(pronounce it carefully)
Positive	pos-i-tive	
Quadrilateral	quad-ri-lat-er-al	
Radius	ra-di-us	
Regular	reg-u-lar	**-lar** (not -ler)
Rhombus	rhom-bus	don't forget **-h-**
Rotation	ro-ta-tion	

Subtraction	sub-trac-tion	
Symmetrical	sym-met-ri-cal	**-y-**, **-mm-**
Triangle	tri-an-gle	**-le**, (not al)
Vertical	ver-tic-al	ending <u>is</u> **-al** this time!
Volume	vol-ume	

Spelling English Related Words

Here are some words that you'll come across in English. Use this chart as a guide to memorise all of them.

Word	**Syllables**	**Difficult Parts**
Advertise	ad-ver-tise	
Advertisement	ad-ver-tise-ment	
Alliteration	al-lit-er-a-tion	remember double l
Apostrophe	a-pos-tro-phe	**-tro- -phe-**
Atmosphere	at-mos-phere	**-ph-**
Chorus	cho-rus	**ch-**
Clause	clause	
Cliche	cli-che	(pronounced cleeshay)
Comparison	com-par-i-son	
Conjunction	con-junc-tion	don't forget 2nd -c-
Consonant	con-so-nant	-so-, -nant- : unclear vowel sounds
Dialogue	di-a-logue	don't forget silent -ue
Expression	ex-pres-sion	double -ss-
Figurative	fig-u-rat-ive	-u-, -a-, unclear vowel sounds
Genre	gen-re	pronounced as the French would say it
Grammar	gram-mar	double **-mm-**

Metaphor	met-a-phor	-ph-
Myth	myth	-y- (not -i-)
Narrator	nar-rat-or	
Onomatopoeia	on-o-mat-o-poei-a	That last but one syllable is somewhat tricky
Pamphlet	pam-phlet	-phlet
Personification	per-son-if-ic-a-tion	easy when you break it up into syllables
Preposition	pre-pos-i-tion	
Playwright	play-wright	don't forget the -w-
Resolution	re-sol-u-tion	
Rhyme	rhyme	Don't forget the -h-
Scene	scene	sc- (like science)
Simile	sim-i-le	-le
Soliloquy	sol-il-o-quy	**-quy**
Synonym	sy-no-nym	sy- and -nym
Tabloid	tab-loid	-loid (noise, voice etc)
Vocabulary	vo-cab-u-lary	pronounce it clearly
Vowel	vow-el	don't forget -e-

Spelling Geography Related Words

Here are some words that you'll come across in Geography. Use this chart as a guide to memorise all of them.

Word	**Syllables**	**Difficult Parts**
Abroad	a-broad	-oa-
Amenity	a-men-i-ty	-men- (sounds like mean)
Authority	au-thor-i-ty	au- (spelt like author)
Climate	cli-mate	-mate: unclear vowel sound

Contour	con-tour	
Country	coun-try	-ou-
Desert	des-ert	only one s
Employment	em-ploy-ment	
Erosion	e-ro-sion	-sion
Estuary	es-tu-a-ry	
Function	func-tion	pronounce it clearly
Habitat	hab-it-at	
Infrastructure	in-fra-struc-ture	easy if you break it into syllables
International	in-ter-na-tion-al	-al unclear vowel sound
Landscape	land-scape	
Latitude	lat-i-tude	
Location	loc-a-tion	
Longitude	long-i-tude	don't forget -g-
Physical	phy-sic-al	phy-
Pollution	pol-lu-tion	double l
Provision	pro-vi-sion	
Regional	re-gion-al	-gion-
Rural	rur-al	
Settlement	set-tle-ment	double t
Situation	sit-u-a-tion	easy if you split it into syllables
Tourist	tour-ist	
Tourism	tour-is-m	pronounce it clearly
Transportation	trans-port-a-tion	syllables!
Urban	ur-ban	ur-
Wealth	weal-th	-ea- unclear vowel sound
Weather	wea-ther	-ea- unclear vowel sound

CHAPTER 8

Improving Spellings with Phonics

Phonics is a system of understanding how letters combine to make sounds and words. You can learn the sound of each letter by associating it with the word that starts with that sound. Phonics skills grow through reading activities, and students learn to distinguish between vowels and consonants and understand letter combinations such as blends and digraphs. Phonics can be great aids for those who want to improve their spellings, as it is through sound that one can write the correct set of alphabets that form the word.

To spell a word correctly that you can pronounce well, look at the following examples:

***Sound:* /iː/**

Example: ***See***

Spellings of Related Words: amoeba, busy, field, key, people, police, scene, see, tea, we

***Sound:* /ɪ/**

Example: ***Ship***

Spellings of Related Words: caesarean, chamois, chassis, coffee, English, exhibit, guilt, lynch, ship, sieve, village

***Sound:* /e/**

Example: ***Bed***

Spellings of Related Words: bed, said, bread, says, guest, bury, leopard, leisure, friend

***Sound:* /æ/**

Example: ***Bad***

Spellings of Related Words: bad, plaid, laugh

***Sound:* /ɑː/**

Example: Calm

Spellings of Related Words: calm, father, heart, bazaar, sergeant, far

***Sound:* /ɒ/**

Example: Pot

Spellings of Related Words: pot, entree, bureaucracy, John, watch, cough, laurel, honest, knowledge

***Sound:* /ɔː/**

Example: Caught

Spellings of Related Words: daughter, ball, board, paw, Paul, four, floor, port, extraordinary, awe, thought, broad, exhaust, exhort, war, bored

***Sound:* /ʊ/**

Example: Put

Spellings of Related Words: put, wood, woman, could

***Sound:* /uː/**

Example: Boot

Spellings of Related Words: boot, do, shoe, group, flew, blue, too, fruit, rude, through, rheumatism, manoeuvre, new, flu, two

Sound: /ʌ/

Example: Cut

Spellings of Related Words: cut, some, does, blood, young

Sound: /ɜː/

Example: Bird

Spellings of Related Words: bird, burn, fern, worm, journal, earn, myrtle, err, colonel

Sound: /ə/

Example: About

Spellings of Related Words: about, fountain, physician, parliament, luncheon, dangerous, nation, restaurant, autumn, sergeant, cupboard, actor, theatre, bigger, surprise, furniture, beggar, soldier, colour, chauffeur, guerrilla, collegiate

Sound: /eɪ/

Example: late

Spellings of Related Words: late, pay, great, vein, weigh, straight, they, gauge, café, fiancée, train, Gaelic, eh

Sound: /əʊ/

Example: go

Spellings of Related Words: go, note, sew, soap, soul, know, toe, oh, brooch, plateau, yeoman, mauve, owe, though, folk, depot

Sound: /aɪ/

Example: like

Spellings of Related Words: like, eye, lie, buy, aye, dye, guide, high, height, aisle, I, my, isle, either, fright

Sound: **/aʊ/**

Example: now

Spellings of Related Words: now, house, plough, hour

Sound: **/ɔɪ/**

Example: boy

Spellings of Related Words: boy, oil, lawyer, buoy

Sound: **/ɪə/**

Example: here

Spellings of Related Words: here, appear, idea, fierce, beer, souvenir, weir, atmosphere, theory

Sound: **/ɛə/**

Example: there

Spellings of Related Words: there, hair, bare, bear, their, prayer, scarce, aerial, mayor, heir, they're

Sound: **/ʊə/**

Example: poor

Spellings of Related Words: poor, cure, tour, cruel, amateur

Sound: **/eɪə/**

Example: player

Spellings of Related Words: player

Sound: **/əʊə/**

Example: lower

Spellings of Related Words: lower, sewer, boa

Sound: **/aɪə/**

Example: fire

Spellings of Related Words: fire, buyer, dyer, tyre, higher, quiet, lion, giant, fiery, tyrant

Sound: **/aʊə/**

Example: tower

Spellings of Related Words: tower, our, hour, Howard

Sound: **/ɔɪə/**

Example: employer

Spellings of Related Words: employer, lawyer, royal

Sound: **/p/**

Example: pen

Spellings of Related Words: pen, happen, shepherd, hope

Sound: **/b/**

Example: back

Spellings of Related Words: back, rubber, cube, raspberry

Sound: **/t/**

Example: tea

Spellings of Related Words: tea, little, Thomas, finished, yacht, debt, late, cigarette, receipt, indict

Sound: **/d/**

Example: day

Spellings of Related Words: day, ladder, called, could, made, I'd

Sound: **/k/**

Example: key

Spellings of Related Words: key, cat, school, biscuit, lock, occur, cheque, talk, lacquer, khaki, quay, trekked, like, clique, saccharine, chocolate

Sound: /g/

Example: go

Spellings of Related Words: go, egg, ghost, league, guard, blackguard

Sound: /ʧ/

Example: chin

Spellings of Related Words: chin, nature, watch, question, cello, Czech, righteous, niche

Sound: /ʤ/

Example: jump

Spellings of Related Words: jump, edge, soldier, age, exaggerate, gradual, adjust, sandwich, gem, judgement

Sound: /f/

Example: few

Spellings of Related Words: few, coffee, cough, photograph, half, often, life, giraffe, sapphire

Sound: /v/

Example: view

Spellings of Related Words: view, of, Stephen, give, halves, I've

Sound: /θ/

Example: thin

Spellings of Related Words: thin

Sound: /ð/

Example: then

Spellings of Related Words: then, bathe

Sound: /s/

Example: soon

Spellings of Related Words: soon, city, nice, psychology, science, pass, schism, listen, sword, promise, pat's, once, psalm, finesse, waltz

Sound: /z/

Example: zero

Spellings of Related Words: zero, is, scissors, anxiety, dazzle, lose, seize, business, clothes

Sound: /ʃ/

Example: she

Spellings of Related Words: she, ocean, sugar, machine, education, tissue, fuchsia, conscious, tension, politician, appreciate, cache

Sound: /ʒ/

Example: measure

Spellings of Related Words: measure, rouge, vision, seizure, usual, equation

Sound: /h/

Example: hot

Spellings of Related Words: hot, whom

Sound: /m/

Example: mat

Spellings of Related Words: mat, lamb, hammer, autumn, calm, government, same, diaphragm, hymn

***Sound:* /n/**

Example: in

Spellings of Related Words: in, know, gnaw, sunny, pneumonia, mnemonic, kitten, certain, cotton, fine, sign, champagne, Wednesday, grandfather, Lincoln

***Sound:* /ŋ/**

Example: sung

Spellings of Related Words: sung, sink, tongue, handkerchief

***Sound:* /l/**

Example: led

Spellings of Related Words: led, ball, battle, pedal, tunnel, pale, gazelle, he'll

***Sound:* /r/**

Example: red

Spellings of Related Words: red, marry, write, rhythm, more, corps, mortgage, you're

***Sound:* /j/**

Example: yet

Spellings of Related Words: yet, onion, beauty, use, new, strenuous, tortilla, queue, vacuum

***Sound:* /w/**

Example: wet

Spellings of Related Words: wet, one, choir, queen, when, suite

***Sound:* /ks/**

Example: box

Spellings of Related Words: box, accept, except, sticks, forks

Sound: **/gz/**

Example: exist

Spellings of Related Words: exist

Sound: **/kʃ/**

Example: luxury

Spellings of Related Words: luxury, anxious

Sound: **/gʒ/**

Example: luxurious

Spellings of Related Words: luxurious

Chapter 9

Spellings with Heteronyms

Heteronyms are words that are spelled the same but have different meanings when pronounced differently. For example, when **Abstract** is pronounced **AB • strakt**, it means summary, but when it is pronounced **ab • STRAKT**, it means some thing that is not like an object.

Heteronyms are specific types of homographs in which the different pronunciations are associated with different meanings. Many heteronyms are the result of one pronunciation being a verb and another being a noun. Since the pronunciation is different, people often get confused and end up writing wrong spellings. Have a look at some common heteronyms, their pronunciation and related meanings.

Word	Pronunciation	Meaning
Ablative	AB • la • tiv	A grammatical case
	a • BLAIT • iv	Tends to ablate (vapourise)
Absent	AB • sent	Missing
	ab • SENT	To keep oneself away
Abstract	AB • strakt	A summary
	ab • STRAKT	Not like an object
Accent	AK • sent	The stress is on bright colours
	ak • SENT	The positive

Acedia	assuh•DEE•uh	A type of fish
	uh•SEED•ia	The deadly sin of sloth
Acuminate	a•KYOO•mi•nut	Pointed
	a•KYOO•mi•nate	To make pointed
Addict	a•DIKT	To cause to become dependent
	AD•ikt	One who is dependent
Address	AD•res	Location
	a•DRES	To specify location or person
Adduct	AD•ukt	A chemical addition product
	a•DUKT	To bring together similar parts
Adept	AD•ept	A highly skilled person
	a•DEPT	Highly skilled
Adulterate	a•DUL•tu•rate	To make impure
	a•DUL•tu•rut	Has engaged in adultery
Advert	AD•vert	Advertisement (British)
	ad•VERT	To refer to casually
Advocate	AD•vu•kut	A lawyer
	AD•vu•kate	To argue in favour of
Aerial	AR•ee•al	Pertaining to aircraft
	ER•ee•al	Antenna
Affect	a•FEKT	To influence
	AF•ekt	The subjective aspect of an emotion
Affiliate	a•FIL•ee•ate	To accept as an associate
	a•FIL•ee•ut	An associate
Affix	a•FIKS	To attach to
	AF•iks	An appendage

Word	Pronunciation	Meaning
Agape	a•GAYP	Wide open
	OG•e•pay	Form of love
Aged	AY•jed	Of an advanced age
	AYJD	To specify the age of a person
Agglomerate	a•GLOM•u•rate	To gather into a ball
	a•GLOM•u•rut	Gathered into a ball
Agglutinate	a•GLOOT•i•nate	To cause to clump together
	a•GLOOT•i•nut	Agglutinative
Aggregate	AG•ri•gate	To gather into a whole
	AG•ri•gut	The whole
Agora	AG•or•uh	A gathering place
	a•gor•AH	Israeli money
Aliment	AL•i•ment	Food
	AL•i•MENT	To give food to
Alloy	AL•oy	Combined metals
	uh•LOY	To mix so as to form an alloy
Ally	ah•LIE	To join with others
	AL•eye	One who is allied
Alternate	ALL•tur•nate	To switch back and forth
	ALL•tur•nut	To change something
Alum	AL•um	Aluminum sulfate
	uh•LUM	Short form of an alumnus
Ana	AN•uh	An equal quantity of each
	AY•nuh	A collection of anecdotes
Analyses	a•NAL•a•seez	Plural of noun analysis
	AN•al•ize•ez	Plural of verb analyse (UK spelling)

Animate	AN•i•mate	To give life to
	AN•i•mut	Living
Annex	a•NEKS or AN•eks	To take for oneself
	AN•eks	An addition to a building
Antedate	ANT•i•date	An assigned date earlier than actual
	ant•i•DATE or ANT•i•date	To assign an earlier date
Appropriate	a•PRO•pree•ate	Take possession of
	a•PRO•pree•ut	Suitable
Approximate	a•PROKS•i•mate	To be nearly the same as
	a•PROKS•i•mut	Nearly correct
Ares	EHRZ	Plural metric unit of area
	EHR•eez	Greek God of war
Arithmetic	a•RITH•mu•tik	One of the three skills other than reading and writing
	ar•ith•MET•ik	As used with scale
Articulate	ar•TIK•u•late	To speak clearly
	ar•TIK•u•lut	One who speaks clearly
As	AZ	Like
	ASS	Roman coin
	AYZ	Plural of a
Aspirate	AS•pi•rate	Inhale
	AS•pi•rut	Material removed by aspiration
Asses	ASS•uz	Plural of ass
	ASS•eez or ASS•uz	Plural of as (the coin)
Associate	as•O•she•ate	Join with
	as•O•she•ut	Whom one is joined with

Ate	AIT	Past of eat
	OT•tee	Reckless ambition
Attaches	uh•TACH•ez	Plural of attach
	at•a•SHAYZ	Plural of attaché
Attenuate	u•TEN•yu•wate	To make thin or slender
	u•TEN•yu•wut	Thin or slender
Attribute	a•TRIB•ewt	Regard as a cause
	AT•ri•bewt	Characteristic feature
Augment	AWG•ment	Lengthened vowel esp. in Greek or Sanskrit verbs
	awg•MENT	To increase
August	AW•gust	Month
	aw•GUS	Admirable
Axes	AK•sez	Plural of ax
	AK•seez	Plural of axis
Ay	AY	Yes (also 'aye')
	EYE	Expressing regret
Bases	BAY•sez	Plural of base
	BAY•seez	Plural of basis
Bass	BASS	Fish
	BAYS	Deep voice
Boule	BOO•lee	Ancient Greek legislative council
	BOOL	Pear-shaped mass with a single crystal
Bow	BAHW	As used with stern
	BOE	As used with arrow
Bowed	BAHWD	To bend something
	BOAD	Referring to something that is already bent

Bower	BAHW•er	A dwelling
	BOE•er	A tenant farmer
Buffet	BUF•et	Hit repeatedly
	bu•FAY	Type of furniture
Bund	BUND	An irrigation embankment
	BOUWND	Federation (usually capitalised)
Bustier	BUS•tee•ur	More busty
	BOOS•tee•ay	Feminine attire
Capo	KAY•poe	Guitar fret clamp
	KAP•oe	Local Mafia boss
Certificate	sur•TIF•i•kut	Document providing authentication
	sur•TIF•u•kate	Testify
Chaps	CHAPS	Fellows
	SHAPS	Leather leggings
Chassis	CHASS•ee	Vehicle undercarriage
	CHASS•eez	Vehicle undercarriages
Close	KLOS	Nearby
	KLOZ	To shut something
Coagulate	ko•AG•u•late	Curdle
	ko•AG•u•lut	That which has coagulated
Coax	KOKES	Persuade
	KOE•ax	Slang for coaxial cable
Collect	ku•LEKT	Gather
	KAWL•ikt	A short prayer
Colon	KOE•lun	":"
	kaw•LOAN	Colonial farmer
	ku•LOAN	Costa Rican monetary unit

Combat	kum•BAT	Fight against
	KOM•bat	Armed battle
Combine	KOM•byn	Association of people
	kum•BYN	To unite
Commune	kuh•MYEWN	With nature
	KOM•yewn	Small collective unit, typically rural
Compact	kum•PAKT	Joined together
	KOM•pakt	To join or pack
Complex	kom•PLEX	Intricate
	KOM•plex	An intricate association
Compound	kum•POWND	Two or major parts
	KOM•pownd	To combine
Compress	kum•PRES	Make smaller
	KOM•pres	Bandage
Concert	KON•sert	Musical performance
	kun•SERT	To plan by mutual agreement
Conduct	kun•DUKT	To guide
	KON•dukt	Behaviour
Confect	kun•FEKT	To put together
	KON•fekt	That which is confected
Confines	kun•FYNZ	Limits
	KON•fynz	The area where something is limited to
Conflict	KON•flikt	A battle
	kun•FLIKT	To fight
Confound	KON•found	Damn
	kun•FOUND	To confuse

Conglomerate	kun•GLOM	Composed of many items •u•rut
	kun•GLOM •e•rate	To gather into a whole
Congregate	KON•gruh•gut	Gathered together
	KON•gruh•gate	To gather together
Congress	KON•gress	A meeting
	kon•GRESS	To assemble
Conjugate	KON•ji•gut	Joined together
	KON•ju•gate	To join together
Conscript	KON•skript	One forced to enroll
	kun•SKRIPT	To force someone to enroll
Conserve	kun•SURV	To preserve with sugar
	KON•surv	A candied fruit
Consociate	kun•SOSH•ee •ut ate or kun• SOSH•ee•	United
	kun•SOSH•ee•ate	To unite
Console	kun•SOLE	Provide solace
	KON•sole	Panel containing controls
Consolidate	kun•SOL•uh•dut or kun•SOL •uh•date	Made firm or solid
	kun•SOL•uh•date	To join together
Consort	KON•sort	Lover
	kun•SORT	To associate with
Construct	kun•STRUKT	Build
	KON•strukt	Something built
Consummate	KON•soo•mut	Extremely skilled
	KON•soo•mate	To complete a

Contact	KON•takt	Electrical connection
	kun•TAKT	To communicate with
Content	KON•tent	What is contained
	kun•TENT	Satisfied
Contest	KON•test	Competition
	kun•TEST	To dispute
Contract	KON•trakt	To agree by signing, etc.
	kun•TRAKT	To get infected by a disease, etc.
Contrary	KON•trer•y	Something that is opposite
	kun•TRER•y	Unruly
Contrast	KON•trast	A difference
	kun•TRAST	To show differences
Converse	KON•vurs	Logic term
	kun•VURS	To talk
Convert	kun•VURT	To change
	KON•vurt	One who has been changed
Convict	kun•VIKT	To find guilty
	KON•vikt	One who has been found guilty
Coop	KOOP	Chicken's home
	KOE•op	Short for cooperative
Coordinate	koe•OR•di•nate	To put in the same order or rank
	koe•OR•di•nut	One that is in the same order or rank
Corps	KOR	A military organisation
	KORZ	Member of military organisation

Covey	KUHV•ee	A group, often of birds
	KOEV•i	A young fellow
Crooked	KROOK•ed	Not straight
	KROOKD	Bent or moved to one side
Cube	KYEWB	A square block
	KYEW•bay	A tropical shrub
Decameter	de•KAM•e•tur	Poetic line with 10 feet
	DEK•a•mee•tur	10 metres
Decrease	di•KREES or DEE•krees	To make it smaller
	DEE•krees or di•KREES	The amount made smaller
Defect	DEE•fekt or di•FEKT	Flaw
	di•FEKT	To desert a cause
Defense	di•FENS	In support of a thing
	DEE•fens or	Act of supporting
Defile	di•FILE	To sully or make dirty
	DEE•file or di•FILE	A narrow passage or gorge
Degenerate	dee•JEN•u•rate	To get worse
	dee•JEN•u•rut	A pervert
Delegate	DEL•i•gate	To pass authority
	DEL•i•gut or DEL•i•gate	A person acting for another
Deliberate	dee•LIB•u•rut	Intentional
	dee•LIB•u•rate	To think carefully
Derogate	DER•o•gate	Disparage
	DER•o•gut or DER•o•gate	Inferior

Desert	DEZ•urt	Dry place
	di•ZURT	Abandon
Desiccate	DES•i•kate	To dry
	DES•i•kut	The product of desiccation
Desolate	DES•u•lut	Barren
	DES•u•late	To make barren
Deviate	DEE•vee•ait	To change direction
	DEE•vee•ut or DEE•vee•ait	Non•normal
Diagnoses	DI•ag•no•sez	To analyse a problem
	di•ag•NO•sees	Identifying the cause of a phenomenon
Diffuse	dif•YOOS	Not concentrated
	dif•YOOZ	To cause to spread thinly
Digest	DIE•jest	A periodical
	die•JEST	To convert food into absorbable substance
Dingy	DIN•jee	Grubby
	DING•ee	Small boat
Discard	DIS•kard	That which has been removed
	dis•KARD	To get rid of
Discharge	dis•CHARJ	To release
	DIS•charj	That which is released
Discord	DIS•kord	A lack of harmony
	dis•KORD	To clash
Discount	DIS•kownt	The amount of the reduction
	dis•KOWNT	To make a deduction
Divers	DIE•vurz	Plural of diver
	die•VURS	Various

Do	DUE	Perform
	DOE	1st note of diatonic scale
Does	DUZ	Auxiliary verb
	DOES	Plural of doe
Dogged	DOG•id	Tenacious
	DOGD	To track or trail persistently
Dove	DOVE	Dived
	DUV	Bird
Drawer	DRAW•ur	One who draws
	DRAWR	Container for items
Duplicate	DUP•li•kut	A copy
	DUP•li•kate	To make a copy
Egress	EE•gres	An exit
	ee•GRES	To exit
Elaborate	i•LAB•u•rut	Rich in detail
	i•LAB•u•rate	Give further detail on
Ellipses	i•LIP•sus	Plural of ellipse
	i•LIP•seez	Plural of ellipsis
Entrance	EN•truns	Door
	in•TRANS	Delight
Envelop	EN•ve•lope	Mail container
	in•VEL•up	To enclose
Epicrisis	e•PIC•ri•sis	Critical literary review
	EP•i•cri•sis	Secondary crisis
Escort	ES•kort	An armed guard
	es•KORT	To accompany
Essay	ES•ay	Piece of writing
	e•SAY or ES•ay	To put to a test

Estimate	ES•ti•mut	A rough calculation
	ES•tu•mate	To make a rough calculation
Evening	EEV•ning	Beginning of night
	EV•un•ing	Levelling out
Ewe	YOO	Female sheep
	AY•way	African language
Excise	EK•size	Type of tax
	ik•SIZE	To cut out
Excuse	ex•KYEWZ	To offer an apology
	ex•KYEWS	An explanation
Exploit	EK•sploit	Feat
	ik•SPLOIT or EX•sploit	Take advantage of
Expose	ik•SPOZE	Reveal
	ek•spoh•ZAY	An exposure of something discreditable
Extract	EK•strakt	Derived from
	il•STRAKT	Remove
Fen	FEN	Marshy ground
	FUN	Chinese money
Ferment	FUR•ment or fur•MENT	A group of living organisms
	fur•MENT	To cause to ferment
Fiasco	fee•AS•koh	Complete failure
	fee•OS•koh	Straw covered bottle
File	FILE	Make smoother
	fi•LAY	A spice
Fillet	fi•LAY	Piece of meat (also "filet")
	FIL•ut	To make into fillets

Fine	FINE	Good or charming
	FEE•nay	Musical term
Forte	FOERT	Strongest part of a blade
	FOR•tay	Loud
Frequent	FREE•kwunt	Often occurring
	free•KWENT	To visit repeatedly
Gill	GIL	Fish organ
	JIL	Unit of volume
Gnome	NOAM	Dwarf like creature
	NO•mee or NOAM	An adage or proverb
Graduate	GRAJ•u•wate	Successfully finish a degree
	GRAJ•u•ut	One who has graduated
Grave	GRAVE	Where you bury someone
	GRAWV•ay	Slowly and solemnly
Hades	HAID•eez	Hell (sometimes capitalised)
	HAIDZ	Angles made by rock faults or veins
Halter	HAWL•tur	Head gear for horses
	HAL•tur	Type of insect wings
Have	HAV	To possess
	HAFF or HAV	To be required
He	HEE	Pronoun
	HAY	5th letter of Hebrew alphabet
Herb	HURB	Man's name
	URB or HURB	Flavourful plant
Hinder	HIN•dur	Hamper
	HINE•dur	To be an obstacle

House	HOWSE	Dwelling
	HOWZ	Give shelter to
Implant	IM•plant	That which has been implanted
	im•PLANT	To place or embed deeply
Import	im•PORT	Bring into a country
	IM•port	That which is brought in
Impress	IM•pres	The mark produced by impressing
	im•PRES	To mark with pressure
Imprint	IM•print	The mark produced by pressure
	im•PRINT	To mark with pressure
Incense	in•SENS	Infuriate
	IN•sens	Perfume for burning
Incline	in•KLINE	To lean towards
	IN•kline	A slope
Incorporate	in•KOR•po•rait	To form into a corporation
	in•KOR•po•rut	Incorporated
Increase	in•KREES	To raise
	IN•krees	A raised position
Indent	in•DENT	To make a notch or depression
	IN•dent	An indentation
Initiate	in•ISH•ee•ate	To begin something
	in•ISH•ee•ut	One who has been initiated
Insert	in•SURT	To put into
	IN•surt	Something inserted
Inset	IN•set	A small item placed within a larger one
	in•SET or IN•set	To make something inset

Instinct	IN•stinkt	A natural impulse
	in•STINKT	Filled with
Insult	IN•sult	A disrespectful remark
	in•SULT	To make a disrespectful remark
Integral	in•TEG•rul	Whole
	INT•i•grul	Expressible in terms of integers
Intercept	in•tur•SEPT	To halt something
	INT•ur•sept	That which has been intercepted
Intermediate	in•tur•MEE•dee•ut	Between
	in•tur•MEE•dee•ate	Intervene
Intern	IN•turn	To restrict
	in•TURN	An internee
Intimate	INT•u•mut	Personal or private
	INT•u•mate	To suggest
Invalid	IN•vu•lud	Incapacitated
	in•VAL•ud	Wrong
Invite	in•VITE	Ask someone to attend
	IN•vite	An invitation
Involute	IN•vuloot	Type of curve
	invul•OOT	To clear up
Isolate	I•so•lait	To set apart from others
	I•so•lut	A product of isolating
Jagged	JAGD	Moved in jerks
	JAG•ud	Having a sharp, uneven edge

Job	JOB	An employement
	JOBE	An affair
Jubilate	JOO•bu•late	Rejoice
	yoo•bu•LAW•tay	Joyous song
Junker	JUNG•kur	Old car
	YOONG•kur	Member of the Prussian aristocracy
Lame	law•MAY	Clumsy
	LAIM	Cripped
Lamed	LAIMD	Made disabled
	LAWM•ed	12th letter of the Hebrew alphabet
Laminate	LAM•u•nate	To combine layers of material
	LAM•u•nut	Composed of layers
Lather	LATHE•ur	Foam
	LAYTH•ur	One who works a lathe
	LATH•ur	One who uses laths
Lead	LED	Heavy metal
	LEED	Show the way
Learned	LURND	Past tense of learn
	LUR•nud	Knowledgeable
Legate	LEG•ut	Official emissary
	li•GATE	Bequeath
Legged	LEG•ud	Having legs
	LEGD	To move
Legitimate	li•JIT•u•mut	Legal or authorised
	li•JIT•u•mate	To make legitimate
Lied	LIED	Past tense of 'lie'
	LEET	German folk song

Lineage	LIN•ee•ij	Descendents of a founder
	LINE•ij	The number of lines of print (also "linage")
Live	LIVE	Full of life; burning
	LIV	To have life
Lower	LOWE•ur	To move down
	LOUW•ur	Frown
Luger	LEW•gur	Pistol
	LEWZH•ur	One who rides a luge
Lunged	LUNJD	Abruptly moved
	LUNGD	Having lungs
Lunger	LUNJ•ur	One that lunges
	LUNG•ur	One that is tubercular
Lupine	LOO•pine	Wolfish
	LOO•pin	Kind of flower
Manes	MAINZ	Plural of mane
	MON•ase	Deified spirits of Roman dead
Mare	MAIR	Female horse
	MAH•ray	Dark area on the moon
Mate	MAIT	Friend
	MAW•tay	South American beverage (maté)
Micrometer	my•KROM•u•tur	Measuring device
	MY•krow•mee•tur	A millionth of a metre
Minute	MIN•ut	60 seconds
	my•NEWT	Wee
Misconduct	mis•KON•dukt	Bad conduct
	mis•kun•DUKT	To misbehave

Mobile	MOWE•beel	Wind•blown sculpture
	MOWE•bul	Movable
Moderate	MOD•u•rut	Not extreme
	MOD•u•rate	To make less extreme
Mole	MOAL	Underground denizen
	MOE•lay	Type of Mexican food
Moped	MOWE•ped	Motorised bike
	MOWEPT	To be gloomy
Mother	MUTH•ur	Mom
	MAWTH•ur	Hunter of moths
Mouse	MOWS	Rodent
	MOWZ	To hunt them
Mouth	MOWTHE	To move one's mouth
	MOWTH	What you speak with
Mow	MAUW	To cut down
	MOWE	A place in a barn
Multiply	MUL•tu•ply	Math operation
	MUL•tu•plee	Manifold
None	NUN	Not any
	NOAN	5th canonical hour
Number	NUM•bur	A numeral
	NUM•ur	More numb
Nun	NUN	Woman in religious order
	NUON	14th letter of Hebrew alphabet
Object	ub•JEKT	Disapprove
	OB•jekt	A material thing
Oblate	a•BLAIT	To make a religious offering
	oh•BLAIT	Flattened at the poles

Obligate	OB•lu•gate	To bind legally or morally
	OB•li•gut	Bound to a restricted lifestyle
Offense	u•FENS	A violation
	OFF•ens	The attacking team
Os	OS	Bone
	OSE	Mouth or orifice
Overage	OH•vur•AIJ	Too old
	OHV•rij	Excess
Overlook	OH•vur•look	Elevated spot with a view
	oh•vur•LOOK	To ignore
Overrun	OH•vur•run	The excess portion
	oh•vur•RUN or OH•vur•run	To run too far
Pace	PAYZS	To set speed
	PAY•SEE	With all due respect to
Palled	PALD	To be buddies with
	PAWLD	Covered with a pall
Palsy	PALL•zee	Trembling disease
	PAL•zee	Friendly
Pan	PAN	Metal container
	PON	A leaf of the betel vine
Pasty	PAY•stee	Paste like
	PASS•tee	A meat pie
Pate	PAIT	Head
	POT	Paste (pâte)
	paw•TAY	Meat spread (pâté)
Patent	PA•tent	Proprietary
	PAY•tent	Unobstructed

Peaked	PEEKD	Sharply pointed
	PEEK•ed	Unhealthy looking
Pedal	PED•il	Place to put your foot
	PEED•il	Relating to the foot
Peer	PEER	One's equal
	PEE•ur	One who pees
Perfect	PUR•fekt	The best possible
	pur•FEKT	To make better
Periodic	pir•ee•OD•ik	Regularly recurring
	pur•eye•od•ik	Table of Elements
Permit	pur•MIT	To allow
	PUR•mit	A pass
Pervert	PUR•vurt	Sexual deviant
	pur•VURT	To corrupt
Pinion	PIN•yun	Part of a bird's wing
	PIN•yown	A pine nut (also "piñon")
Pique	PEEK	To stimulate
	PEE•kay	A type of tick
Placer	PLAY•sur	One of the winners in a competition
	PLAS•ur	Mineral deposit
Plies	PLYZ	Plural of ply
	plee•AZE	Plural of plié
Poise	POYZ	Easy composure
	PWOZ	Unit of measurement for viscosity
Polish	POE•lish	From Poland
	POL•ish	Rub
Poll	POLE	A casting of votes
	PAWL	Pass degree

Postulate	POS•cha•lait	To claim as true
	POS•cha•lat or POS•cha•lait	That which is claimed to be true
Prayer	PRAY•ur	One who prays
	PRER	A request made to god
Precedent	PRESS•uh•dent	Authoritative example
	pree•SEE•dent or PRESS•uh•dent	What came before this
Precipitate	pri•SIP•u•tate	To rain or snow
	pri•SIP•ut•ut	A solid separated from a solution
Predicate	PRED•i•kut	Part of a sentence
	PRED•i•kate	To assert or declare
Premise	PREM•us	A statement
	pri•MIZE or PREM•us	To state in advance
Present	pri•ZENT	Give
	PREZ•ent	A gift
Primer	PRIM•ur or PRY•mur	Intro book for teaching
	PRY•mur	Used for priming
Proceeds	pro•SEEDZ	Continues
	PRO•seedz	Income
Process	pru•SESS	Move in a procession
	PRAW•sess	The method
Produce	pru•DOOS	Create
	PROD•oos	Fruits and veggies
Progress	PROG•rus	Movement towards a goal
	pru•GRES	To advance

Project	PRAW•ject	Undertaking
	pru•JEKT	Hurl
Prospect	prus•PEKT	Explore
	PROS•pekt	A likely candidate
Protest	PRO•test	Display of disapproval
	pru•TEST	To object to
Pussy	POOS•ee	A Cat
	PUS•ee	Full of pus
Putting	PUTT•ing	Golfing
	POOT•ing	Placing
Ragged	RAGD	Tormented
	RAG•ud	Tattered
Raven	RAY•vun	Black bird
	RAV•un	To devour greedily
Re	REE or RAY	With regard to
	RAY	2nd note of diatonic scale
Read	REED	To apprehend or have knowledge
	RED	Already apprehended
Real	REEL	Actual
	ray•OL	Former Spanish money
Rebel	ri•BEL	To resist
	REB•ul	One who rebels
Rebound	REE•bound	To spring back
	REE•BOUND	To recover from a setback
Recall	REE•kawl	To call back
	ree•KAWL	The act of recalling
Recap	REE•kap	A recapped tire
	ree•KAP	To put new tread on a tire

Recess	REE•ses	A nook
	ri•SES	To put something into a recess
Recitative	REH•sih•TAY•tiv	Relating to recital
	REH•sih•tuh•TEEV	An opera style that emphasizes dialogue
Recoil	ri•KOIL	To flinch or wince
	REE•koil	The kickback of a gun
Recollect	rek•a•LEKT	Remember
	REE•kol•ekt	To collect again
Record	REK•urd	A report or instrument
	ri•KORD	To register
Recount	REE•cownt	To count again
	ree•COWNT	To give a detailed account of
Recover	REE•kuver	To cover again
	ree•KUVER	Retrieve
Recreate/ion	REK•ree•ate	Relax
	REE•kree•ATE	Create again
Redo	REE•DUE	Do again
	REE•due or REE•DUE	Redecorate
Redress	ri•DRES	Compensate
	REE•dress or ri•DRES	Compensation
	REE•DRES	Dress again
Refill	REE•fill	A replenishment
	ree•FILL	Fill again
Refit	ree•FIT	To fit out or resupply
	REE•fit	The act of refitting

Reflex	REE•fleks	An automatic action
	REE•FLEKS	Flex again
Reform	ri•FORM	Change for the better
	REE•FORM	Form again
Refund	ri•FUND	To return money
	REE•fund	The returned money
Refuse	ri•FUSE	Do not accept
	REF•yoos	Garbage
Regenerate	ri•JEN•ur•ait	To generate or produce anew
	re•JEN•ur•ut	Formed or created again
Regress	ri•GRES	To go back
	REE•gres	The act of reasoning backwards
Rehash	REE•hash	The act of rehashing
	ree•HASH	To work up in a new form
Reject	REE•jekt	One that has been rejected
	ree•JEKT	To refuse to accept
Relapse	ri•LAPS	Fall back
	REE•laps	The act of relapse
Relay	REE•lay	Electrical switch
	ri•LAY	Pass on
Release	ree•LEES	Let go
	REE•LEES	Lease again
Remake	REE•make	Which is remade
	REE•MAKE	To make again
Repair	ree•PAIR	Fix
	REE•PAIR	Pair again

Repatriate	ri•PAY•tree•ait	To return someone to their country
	re•PAY•tree•ut	Someone who has been returned
Repent	ri•PENT	Regret
	REE•punt	Creeping
Replay	REE•play	A repetition
	ree•PLAY	Play again
Report	ree•PORT	An account
	REE•PORT	To relate
Represent	rep•ri•ZENT	Stand for
	REE•pri•ZENT	Present again
Repress	ri•PRES	Push back
	REE•PRES	Press again
Reprint	REE•print	A reprinted object
	REE•PRINT	Print again
Reprise	ri•PRIZE	A resumption of action
	ri•PREEZ	A musical repetition
Reproof	ri•PROOF	Rebuke
	REE•PROOF	Reread
Rerun	REE•run	A second showing
	REE•RUN	Run again
Research	ri•SURCH	Investigate
	REE•SURCH	Search again
Reseda	ri•SED•u	Type of flower
	RAY•zu•da	Grayish-green colour
Resent	ree•ZENT	Be indignant
	REE•SENT	Sent again

Reserve	ri•ZURV	Hold back
	REE•SURV	Serve again
Reside	ree•ZIDE	To dwell
	REE•SIDE	To give a new siding
Resign	ri•ZINE	Quit
	REE•SIGN	Sign again
Resolve	ri•ZOLV	Settle dispute
	REE•SOLV	Solve again
Resort	ri•ZORT	Vacation spot
	REE•SORT	Sort again
Resound	ree•ZOUND	To echo with sound
	REE•SOUND	To sound again
Restore	ri•STOR	To rebuild
	REE•STOR	To place back
Resume	ri•ZOOM	Continue
	REZ•oo•may	Work summary (also résumé)
Retable	REE•tabe•ul	Placed on the agenda again
	ri•TABE•ul	Shelf behind an alter
Retake	ree•TAKE	To take again
	REE•take	Tha act of retaking
Retard	REE•tard	Mentally slow person
	ri•TARD	To make slow
Return	ri•TURN	Revert or give back
	REE•TURN	Redo something
Review	ri•VEW	Look over
	REE•VEW	View something again
Rewind	ree•WINED	Wind again
	REE•wined	The act of rewinding

River	RI•vur	Flowing water
	RIE•vur	One who splits wood
Rose	ROZE	Type of flower
	roze•AY	Type of wine
Rout	ROUT	Disastrous defeat
	ROTE	A cattle bellow
Router	ROUT•ur	Woodworking tool
	ROOT•ur	A horse trained for distance races
Row	RAU	A fight
	ROE	To propel a vessel, especially a boat
Rugged	RUG•id	Sturdy
	RUGD	Pulled or torn
Sake	SAKE	Cause
	SOK•ee	Japanese drink (also "saki")
Salve	SAV	Ointment
	SALV	Salvage
Secrete/d/ive	SEE•krut	To conceal in a hiding place
	si•KREET	To form and give off
Seer	SEE•ur or SIR	One that sees
	SIR	Unit of weight
Segment	SEG•munt	A portion
	seg•MENT	To separate into segments
Separate	SEP•u•rate	Distinct
	SEP•u•rut	Set apart
Sewer	SUE•ur	An artificial conduct
	SOE•ur	One who sews

Sheave	SHEEV	To pull the oars in reverse
	SHIV	A grooved wheel
Shin	SHIN	Part of leg
	SHEEN	22nd letter in Hebrew alphabet
Shower	SHAU•ur	Bathe
	SHOW•ur	One who shows
Sin	SIN	Moral offense
	SEEN or Sin	21st letter in Hebrew alphabet
Singer	SING•ur	One who sings
	SINJ•ur	One who singes
Skied	SKEED	Past tense of ski
	SKYD	Hung a painting up high
Slaver	SLAY•vur	One who sells slaves
	SLAV•ur	Drool
Slough	SLUE	Marshy place
	SLUF	Shed skin
Sol	SOLE	Syllable of the fifth tone of a diatonic scale
	SAWL	Old French coin
Soles	SOULZ	Plural of sole
	SOH•lase	Plural of sol (French coin)
Sow	SAU	Female pig
	SOH	Plant seeds
Stabile	STAY•beel	Abstract sculpture
	STAY•bil	Steady
Stingy	STINJ•ee	Reluctant to spend
	STING•ee	Able to sting

Stipulate	STIP•yu•late	Request explicitly
	STIP•yu•lut	Having stipules
Subject	SUB•jikt	One who is ruled by another
	sub•JEKT	To subjugate
Supply	su•PLY	Provide
	SUP•lee	In a supple way
Survey	SUR•vay	Inspect
	sur•VAY	A report of what has been surveyed
Suspect	sus•PEKT	To doubt
	SUS•pekt	A suspected person
Swinger	SWING•ur	One who swings
	SWIN•jur	Whopper
Syndicate	SIN•di•kut	A business group
	SIN•du•kate	To sell to a syndicate
Tang	TANG	Sharp flavour
	TONG	Chinese dynasty
Tarry	TAIR•ee	Linger
	TAR•ee	Covered with tar
Taxes	TAK•suz	Plural of tax
	TAK•seez	Plural of taxis
Taxis	TAK•seez	Plural of taxi
	TAK•sus	Manual reduction of a hernia
Tear	TAIR	Rip
	TEER	Produced when crying
Tester	TES•tur	One who tests
	TEES•tur	Canopy over a bed
Thou	THEOW	You
	THOW	A thousand

Tier	TEER	Row or rank
	TIE•ur	One who ties
Toots	TOOTS	Blows a horn
	TUHTS	Short for Tootsie (slang)
Tori	TOR•ee	A large convex molding
	TOR•eye or TOR•ee	Plural of torus
Torment	TOR•ment	Agony
	tor•MENT	To cause agony
Tower	TAO•ur	Tall building
	TOE•ur	One who tows
Transect	trans•EKT	To cut across
	TRANS•ekt	A sample strip of vegetation
Transfer	trans•FUR	To move
	TRANS•fur	A transference
Transplant	trans•PLANT	To move to another place
	TRANS•plant	The act of transplanting
Transport	trans•PORT	To carry
	TRANS•port	The act of transporting
Transpose	trans•POZE	To transform
	TRANS•poze	Matrix formed by swapping rows and columns
Trepan	tri•PAN	To remove a core
	TREE•pan	Heavy tool used in mining
Tropic	TRAW•pick	Parallels of latitude on globe
	TROW•pick	Influencing the activity of
Tush	TUSH	A tooth
	TOUWSH	Your fanny
Upset	UP•set	Out of order
	up•SET	Angry

Use	YOOS	Purpose
	YOOZ	To consume
Used	YOOST	A thing in past
	YOOSED	Consumed
Vice	VISE	An immoral habit
	VIE•see	A turn in sequence
Viola	vie•OH•la	Flower
	vee•OH•la	Musical instrument
Violist	VIUL•ist	Viol player
	vee•OH•lust	Viola player
Whiffler	WIF•lur	One that clears the way for a procession
	WIF•e•lur	One that changes his opinion
Wicked	WIK•id	Shrewd
	WIKD	Has one or more wicks
Wind	WIND	Moving air
	WINED	Turn
Winded	WIN•ded	Out of breath
	WINE•ded	Blew a horn
Withy	WITHE•ee	A flexible slender twig
	WITH•ee	Flexibly tough
Won	WAHN	Korean currency
	WUN	Past tense of win
Wound	WOOND	Injury
	WOWND	Past tense of wind
Yak	YAK	Long haired ox
	YAUK or YAK	Laugh (slang)
Ye	YEE	Plural of than
	YUH or THE or YEE	Archaic of you

CHAPTER 10

Commonly Misspelled Words

Have a quick look at the commonly misspelled words. Not all of them are wrong. Try to spell the misspelled words correctly and match your answers with the correct spellings given on next page.

Misspelled Words

Awhil	Abcence	Accelerate	Accomplish
Accumullate	Acknowlege	Acquiantance	Acquire
Acrross	Afficionado	Aniont	Appology
Axl	Accardion	Barbeque	Begining
Brocoli	Bussiness	Camuoflage	Candi date
Cantalope	Carbaretor	Caribbean	Cartillage
Chauvanism	Chilli	Chocolati	Coliseum
Colonell	Commemarate	Congratulations	Coolly
Critisize	Dalmatain	Decieve	Deffendant
Defiant	Desiccate	Desparate	Deterrence
Devlopment	Diorama	Disappear	Disappoint
Dissipatte	Difference	Exstasy	Especifically
Exsellent	Exersise	Explanation	Farenheit
Finaly	Flabberghast	Flotation	Fourth
Fulfill	Generaly	Genuis	Government
Grammer	Gross	Gutttural	Handkerchief
Horriffic	Hipocrisy	Imittate	Inadverttent

Incidentaly
Incredible
Ingeniuos
Irrascible
Irresisstible
Knowledghe
Labelled
Led
Laison
Lieutenant
Liquefy
Lose
Lieng
Magicaly
Marshmalow
Mischeif
Misoghoyny
Misile
Nauseos
Necesary
Noone
Occahsion
Occur/occurred
Octopus
Officiale
Onomatopoiea
Parallel
Parlaiment
Peice
Peninsula
Paraoh
Physical
Plenitude
Pigoen
Pistachio
Plaesant
Propogate
Preferable
Presumptous
Proseed
Razpberry
Pooerile
Purusue
Putrefy
Rememberance
Reciept
Refrigerator
Religios
Salary
Renowned
Ridiculus
Sacrilegios
Scissorss
Sandal
Sandwhich
Savy
Septuageanarian
Sieze
Sensible
Separate
Similar
Sheriff
Shish kebab
Siige
Semile
Special
Subpoena
Success
Tongue
Tablaeu
Tarif
Tommorro
Ukulele
Too/to/two
Tragedy
Truly
Withhold
Ussage
Viceous
Village
You're/your

Correct Spellings

A while
Absence
Accelerate
Accomplish
Accumulate
Acknowledge
Acquaintance
Acquire
Across
Aficionado
Anoint
Apology
Axle
Accordion
Barbecue
Beginning
Broccoli
Business
Camouflage
Candidate
Cantaloupe
Carburetor
Caribbean
Cartilage

Chauvinism	Chili	Chocolaty	Coliseum
Colonel	Commemorate	Congratulations	Coolly
Criticize	Dalmatian	Deceive	Defendant
Defiant	Desiccate	Desperate	Deterrence
Development	Diorama	Disappear	Disappoint
Dissipate	Difference	Ecstasy	Especially
Excellent	Exercise	Explanation	Fahrenheit
Finally	Flabbergast	Flotation	Fourth
Fulfil	Generally	Genius	Government
Grammar	Gross	Guttural	Handkerchief
Horrific	Hypocrisy	Imitate	Inadvertent
Incidentally	Incredible	Ingenious	Irascible
Irresistible	Knowledge	Labeled	Led
Liaison	Lieutenant	Liquefy	Lose
Lying	Magically	Marshmallow	Mischief
Misogyny	Missile	Nauseous	Necessary
No one	Occasion	Occur/occurred	Octopus
Official	Onomatopoeia	Parallel	Parliament
Piece	Peninsula	Pharaoh	Physical
Plenitude	Pigeon	Pistachio	Pleasant
Propagate	Preferable	Presumptuous	Proceed
Raspberry	Puerile	Pursue	Putrefy
Remembrance	Receipt	Refrigerator	Religious
Salary	Renowned	Ridiculous	Sacrilegious
Scissors	Sandal	Sandwich	Savvy
Septuagenarian	Seize	Sensible	Separate
Similar	Sheriff	Shish kebab	Siege

Simile	Special	Subpoena	Success
Tongue	Tableau	Tariff	Tomorrow
Ukulele	Too/to/two	Tragedy	Truly
Withhold	Usage	Vicious	Village
You're/your			